T0079746

LAMB

Edible

Series Editor: Andrew F. Smith

EDIBLE is a revolutionary series of books dedicated to food and drink that explores the rich history of cuisine. Each book reveals the global history and culture of one type of food or beverage.

Already published

Apple Erika Janik *Barbecue* Jonathan Deutsch and Megan J. Elias *Beef* Lorna Piatti-Farnell *Beer* Gavin D. Smith
Brandy Becky Sue Epstein *Bread* William Rubel
Cake Nicola Humble *Caviar* Nichola Fletcher
Champagne Becky Sue Epstein *Cheese* Andrew Dalby
Chocolate Sarah Moss and Alexander Badenoch
Cocktails Joseph M. Carlin *Curry* Colleen Taylor Sen
Dates Nawal Nasrallah *Doughnut* Heather Hunwick
Dumplings Barbara Gallani *Eggs* Diane Toops
Figs David C. Sutton *Game* Paula Young Lee
Gin Lesley Jacobs Solmonson *Hamburger* Andrew F. Smith
Herbs Gary Allen *Hot Dog* Bruce Kraig *Ice Cream* Laura B.
Weiss *Lamb* Brian Yarvin *Lemon* Toby Sonneman
Lobster Elisabeth Townsend *Milk* Hannah Velten
Mushroom Cynthia D. Bertelsen *Nuts* Ken Albala
Offal Nina Edwards *Olive* Fabrizia Lanza *Oranges* Clarissa
Hyman *Pancake* Ken Albala *Pie* Janet Clarkson
Pineapple Kaori O' Connor *Pizza* Carol Helstosky
Pork Katharine M. Rogers *Potato* Andrew F. Smith
Pudding Jeri Quinzio *Rice* Renee Marton *Rum* Richard Foss
Salmon Nicolaas Mink *Sandwich* Bee Wilson *Sauces* Maryann
Tebben *Sausage* Gary Allen *Soup* Janet Clarkson
Spices Fred Czarra *Sugar* Andrew F. Smith *Tea* Helen Saberi
Tequila Ian Williams *Truffle* Zachary Nowak *Vodka* Patricia
Herlihy *Water* Ian Miller *Whiskey* Kevin R. Kosar
Wine Marc Millon

Lamb

A Global History

Brian Yarvin

REAKTION BOOKS

To my wife, a woman who always loves a well-braised lamb shank

Published by Reaktion Books Ltd
33 Great Sutton Street
London EC1V ODX, UK

www.reaktionbooks.co.uk

First published 2015

Copyright © Brian Yarvin 2015

Printed and bound in China by Toppan Printing Co. Ltd

A catalogue record for this book is available
from the British Library

ISBN 978 1 78023 499 1

Contents

Introduction

What is it about lamb? It is the meat of choice for ambitious chefs and cooking-show contestants, yet there are carnivores who just will not touch it. Somehow, for some reason, lamb is an emotive meat. It is not this way everywhere; lamb is consumed with gusto in South Asia and is found in every British high-street butcher shop.

Today, the very sight of sheep grazing tells us we've left the sprawl of modern life and reached a place where people are continuing ancient traditions of working with nature. In North America, vendors of lamb meat, sheep's milk cheese and even locally produced wool are returning to contemporary farmers' markets.

What exactly is lamb? It is the meat of sheep that are slaughtered before they reach the age of one. This results in a fraction of the amount of meat you would get from a pig, a cow or, for that matter, an adult sheep. Not only is this meat of very high quality, but it can be raised easily on very small patches of land. Lamb is the perfect meat for the modern small farmer.

Lamb is perfectly suited to small-scale farming for the very same reasons the first farmers appreciated it: it is relatively easy to raise and sells well. Not only do sheep eat grass, but

Ram at Dayspring Farm in Vermont.

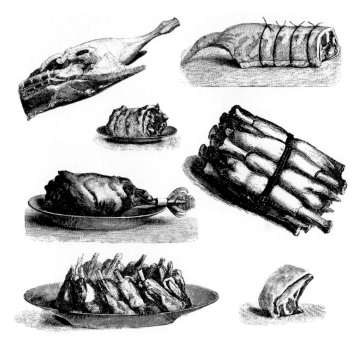

Engraving of a collection of seven lamb dishes from *Le livre de cuisine* (1874) by Jules Goufe.

they can make a big meal from a small patch of it. They do not need to roam far and wide, as cows do, and do not require extra feed the way pigs do.

Lamb is not the only sheep meat eaten by humans. Mutton, the meat of sheep slaughtered after the age of one, was once popular everywhere. Today, it remains so in Africa, parts of Asia and Latin America, while Britain is having a serious mutton revival – complete with an endorsement for its consumption from the Prince of Wales. Still, lamb is more popular by far. You'll find lamb in soups and stews and on skewers and barbecue grills. Close your eyes and imagine a plate of grilled lamb chops in an alpine village *trattoria*, a bowl of spicy lamb noodle soup at a Xi'an street stall, a deep-fried lamb samosa in a Pakistani restaurant or those grilled mutton kidneys that James Joyce spoke of, with butter, salt and pepper . . . lamb is the true global red meat.

Lamb is food, metaphor and mythology. Since the domestication of sheep almost 10,000 years ago, lamb has found its

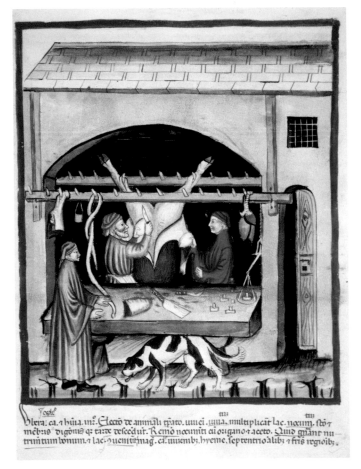

'Butchery', from the *Tacuinum sanitatis* (Handbook of Health), 14th century.

Sheep grazing at Burningheart Farm in New Jersey.

way into scripture, literature and culture: think of the Golden Fleece, Blood of the Lamb or *The Lamb Lies Down on Broadway*. So let's sit down and take a look at just what lamb is and how it got that way. It is quite a story.

I

Basics: Sheep and Lamb

Ten or eleven thousand years ago, a hunting party heard a strange bleating sound. It was unlikely to be familiar: the wild sheep they had been stalking were not only shy, but spent most of their time high in the mountains on rocky terrain on which humans were not too comfortable.

Realizing that what they heard was an injured animal, they crept towards it quietly, thinking, 'Here's an easy meal.' Moments later, they found themselves staring at a suffering, pregnant sheep. At first, they were going to put the animal out of its misery on the spot, but they soon had the idea of bringing it to camp and nursing it back to health – and why not? If the sheep gave birth, they would save themselves another hunt; if it died, they would still have an animal's worth of meat. They took the poor sheep back and soon they had it and a couple of baby ones as well. Those hunters were the proud owners of the first domestic lambs.

Once those lambs were born, the hunters saw a wholly different animal. Docile, and almost obedient, they were easy to keep and formed herds that would stay together without much pressure from the outside. The only problem was breeding those first lambs in captivity. Should they capture more animals for diversity's sake or just mate brothers and sisters?

Domesticating and breeding sheep – indeed, growing versus gathering anything – would have been a decision more than a discovery. Certainly, our ancestors knew how both plants and animals reproduced long before they themselves attempted to control the process. So there could have been another scenario: one day, a group of hunters chased a female sheep and cornered her. While it was their habit to go in for the kill, this time they decided to bring her home alive. With a bit more effort, they could capture a live male, too, and if they put the two together, they could have more sheep without needing to hunt. Certainly it would be more efficient if they captured some live sheep, allowed them to breed and reaped the harvest, rather than hunting and killing the animals one at a time.

Whatever the earliest domesticators did, we have to wonder what they were thinking. Did they expect to keep just a few animals? Did they imagine a large herd? Did they build a pen first? Could they have guessed that a whole new profession would spring up around sheep raising? And did they have any inkling of how to get formerly wild animals to mate? Captive breeding might not have worked the first time, but sheep are not all that difficult to mate and success may have come fairly quickly.

And did they already know about lamb as a food? Had they noticed that the meat of smaller, younger animals had better flavour and was more tender? Our hunters had no way of recording their opinions. They existed thousands of years before the first recipes or cookbooks – indeed, thousands of years before the first written words.

As well as being hunters, they were certainly gatherers. There's plenty of evidence that they ate grains, though none that tells us if they gathered grains or grew them. The archaeological record shows that people developed farming methods and domesticated sheep during roughly the same era and in

Relief of a figure making an offering of a lamb, from the Darius Palace in Persepolis, Iran, 5th century BCE.

pretty much the same place – but it does not tell us which happened first. It appears that this added up to a culture that ate a balanced diet of meats, grains and vegetables, but was only just learning how to produce and preserve it; nobody really knows if it happened exactly that way or not, but somehow, someone managed to domesticate sheep and make the move from hunter to farmer. First, a steady supply of meat and then, after they got to know the animals better, the farmers started making thread, rope and bowstrings from the sinews, the hair became wool and the skin first became hides, then leather and parchment. Even the fat was useful: it could be made into a balm for healing or tallow for candles. With a bit more effort and some creative combining, you can create food, medicine, clothing, shoes, containers, rugs and tents from sheep.

These domesticated sheep were tame enough to be milked and, with that, there was a beverage, followed by yogurt and cheese. In one way, these early sheep were even easier than our own today: they did not need shearing. Ancient breeds of sheep shed their outer coats of fine fibre twice a year. And there was more to be had: the horns made fine drinking vessels and musical instruments too. All you had to do was lead a sheep to a patch of grass. It was enough to lift us out of the Stone Age, and made hunting and gathering look just a bit old fashioned.

Sheep did not come with an instruction book. It was not until they were kept in captivity that somebody thought of collecting the woollen fibres while the animals were alive, rather than just wearing their hairy skins, removed whole from the dead animal. And there was one act that required a different sort of courage: who was the first person to drink a sheep's milk? Every detail of their raising and harvesting had to be figured out by probably painful trial and error, including the big question: for maximum flavour, texture and economy, when do you slaughter the animals?

The older, adult wild sheep that those hunter-gatherers caught were full of flavour, but they were also hard to find and the meat tough to chew. The animals they raised themselves

Grazing sheep at Dayspring Farm in Vermont.

turned out to be a different story: milder, more tender and, eventually, happy to reproduce under the watchful eyes of shepherds – an entirely new occupation that sprang up as sheep husbandry took root.

It was not such a bad deal for the sheep, either. In the care of humans, they could thrive in a way they could not in the wild. Their wounds and illnesses were nursed and they were led to the best grazing land. Shepherds and dogs did a pretty good job of protecting them from predators, too. Some sheep may have returned to the wild, but for the most part it seems they embraced their new role as the world's first farm animals.

We might still be guessing about how the first sheep were domesticated, but it is pretty certain where it took place: in the Zagros Mountains of Iran. With peaks in the range of 4,300 m (14,000 ft) high, the Zagros can be thought of as an arid version of the Rockies or the Alps. They provided the sort of rough terrain and patchy grass that both sheep and shepherds love.

With a steady supply of both wild and domesticated sheep to learn from, those early herdsmen started to study what they had. We all know the basics: sheep have four legs and a hairy coat and make a distinctive 'baa' sound. The farmers also knew that sheep could grow big and strong eating nothing but grass. Clearly, they were quite different from dogs – the only other animal they kept; sheep did not try to be friendly with humans or help in the way dogs did – they just went about their business, producing meat, milk and wool.

Modern re-creation of the Larsa tablet bouillon recipe.

Unlike dogs, sheep did not compete with people for food at all. Dogs may have begged for food, but sheep keep to themselves. Indeed, all an early farmer would have needed to raise sheep was a bit of patchy grassland. And when the grass was finished, the animals just moved on to ... well ... greener pastures. Sheep were such good harvesters that early examples of the first agricultural tool, the sickle, resembled a sheep's jaws, with tiny blades placed like teeth. It was the first – but not the last – time that sheep acted as a model.

Back then, sheep comprised practically the whole farm; their flesh, milk, hides, sinews and horns were the only animal agricultural products that existed. When it came to crops like barley and wheat, sheep did their part too, by providing fertilizer. It was official: *Ovis aries*, the sheep, of mountain crags, pastures and parent of the lamb, had been domesticated.

Today, regulatory bodies such as the European Union and the American Food and Drug Administration (FDA) proffer strict definitions of 'lamb' and 'mutton'; indeed, some countries even include an in-between category called 'hogget', for sheep too old to be called 'lamb' and too young to be 'mutton'. This has not always been the case. Although those first shepherds in Larsa, Mesopotamia (today's Iraq), may have slaughtered their lambs when they were one year old, the age prescribed by the FDA, the rest of history shows far less consistency in the matter. Sometimes we see clues: one historical record might describe a meal that consisted of a whole roast lamb that provided enough meat for only four people, while another source describes a lamb that fed twenty. Then again, some farm and kitchen records detail the ages and weights of slaughtered animals with the greatest precision. And there are times when we just do not know if an original recipe was for what would today be an adult sheep or a baby lamb.

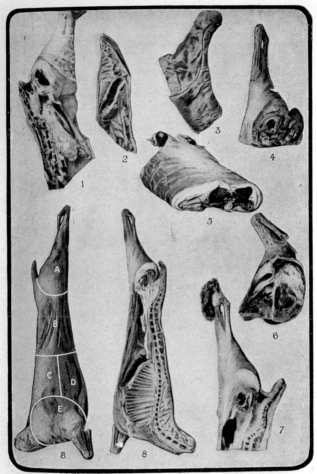

1. Hind-quarter.   2. Breast.   3. Neck.   4. Leg.   5. Saddle.   6. Shoulder.
7. Haunch.   8. Side: A. Leg,   B. Loin,   C. Best End of Neck,   D. Breast,
E. Shoulder, F. Scrag.

'Various Cuts of Mutton', from Mrs Beeton's *Book of Household Management* (1907 edition).

There would be no lamb without sheep; and, for the most part, 'lamb' refers to our modern way of eating them. Though there are some people who go for mutton, the flesh of grown-up sheep, the meat of young animals – as lamb chops, lamb shanks, leg of lamb or lamb shoulder, and maybe a bit of minced lamb – tends to be how we eat sheep today.

2
Lamb: A Culinary History

Imagine a wooden shed sheltering a couple of lambs. Nearby, our early herdsmen were making a fire for warmth. Suddenly, a spark flew out and ignited the shed. At first, the herdsmen wanted to rush in and rescue the animals. Then the smell of roasting meat reached them. Cooking had been discovered.

This story is not historical fact, but it is taken seriously as a theory by many anthropologists. Somebody, somewhere had to be the first person deliberately to put meat on a fire and invent cooking. Other experts believe that in some places it may have happened long before the domestication of sheep, and in others, long after. In order to know the history of lamb though, we have to learn not only the story of shepherding, but that of cooking too.

Lamb bones have been found scattered around the campfires of the earliest farmers. At Shanidar, in northern Iraq's Zagros Mountains, sheep were slaughtered at the age of one. This is not a coincidence: people across most of the world do the very same thing today. From that time, 9,000 years ago, 'lamb' has been defined this way. Soon afterwards, lamb began to make the move from animal to ingredient and evolve into the widely consumed meat we see today. When did it become curry, kebabs and Lancashire hotpot?

A pot of *navarin printanier*, the classic French lamb stew.

Those first cooks in the Zagros Mountains were not all that sophisticated; roasting seems to be the only cooking method they knew. It was to be thousands of years before boiling, frying, sautéing and stewing were invented. Still, lamb roasted over an open fire was a favourite, as the stacks of butchered, charred bones that have been found in their settlements will attest.

The world's earliest written recipes, on clay tablets dating from the seventeenth century BCE, from Larsa in southern Mesopotamia, include one for a herbaceous soup or 'lamb bouillon'. It was made from crumbed cereal cake, onion, coriander (cilantro), cumin, leeks and garlic. This dish appears to be more similar to a modern braised stew than a bouillon of today – a clear or golden broth, or even those salty little cubes that people use to make soup over a campfire. Two thousand years later, the Roman recipe collection known as *Apicius* contained a whole chapter of lamb recipes; its 'Lamb and Beans' was a forerunner of what we would now think of as rustic French cuisine.

Set down thousands of years after those bones were roasted in the Zagros Mountains, the Larsa recipe for lamb bouillon gives us a pretty good sense of how people were eating lamb. It does not give cooking times, but there is enough information to infer a wet method and a long simmer. As for the other ingredients – onion, coriander, cumin, leeks and garlic – these are common in the region's cooking today. That leaves 'crumbled cereal cake'. These were preserved bricks of whole, unground grain. Added to a simmering broth, they would function as a thickener, textural complement and flavour accent. Cereal cake is not something that is

Lamb of God (Agnus Dei), half-relief on the wall of the atrium of St Euphrasius Church, Poreč, Croatia.

consumed in the same form in the region today, yet the other ingredients probably still taste about the same as they did in those ancient days.

Were the people of Larsa eating something similar to a modern Scottish lamb broth, or 'Scotch broth'? It seems that way; cumin and coriander might not be traditionally used in the Highlands, but onions and leeks certainly are. And while Scots might not eat crumbled cereal cake, the barley used in Scotch broth plays the same role.

It was not long before the Mesopotamians added beef, goat, ducks and geese to their farmyards. This did not stop them from enjoying lamb, though: they raised it and ate it, and when they encountered other people, encouraged them to raise lambs too.

To the east, not far from Mesopotamia, the diet of the ancient Egyptians was not all that different. Of course, New World ingredients that are common in Middle Eastern cooking today, such as potatoes, chillies and tomatoes, weren't yet introduced to the region. Still, there were plenty of ingredients to choose from; the ancient Egyptians cooked their lamb with spices such as coriander, cumin and garlic. Vegetables, including okra (ladies' fingers), leeks and onions, and chickpeas, were a staple; eaten along with starches like wheat and barley, all this made for an interesting and flavourful diet. Artwork from the period shows food being cooked in tall, narrow-necked vessels that look surprisingly like elongated tagines, a clay cooking pot common in North Africa today in which stews are typically made, often including lamb as a primary ingredient.

In Egypt's Nile valley, raising sheep was pretty much as it was in Mesopotamia. Flocks could be kept in the same general area all year; there was no need to bring the animals up into the mountains in the summer and down again in the

Jesus Christ as the Good Shepherd, from an early Christian floor mosaic at the Basilica of Aquileia, Italy.

cold of winter. It was a truly agrarian society, where hunting and gathering were relegated to minor roles.

Readers of the holy books will be familiar with the many lamb and sheep metaphors contained therein. And while those images may be very powerful, it is the story of Exodus from the Hebrew Bible that actually tells us about lamb eating. At this time, sheep and goats were the livestock of choice, and lamb was a sacrificial animal and staple meat. Exodus tells how the Hebrew people left Egypt and made their way to the Promised Land. Not only did they take their flocks of sheep with them, their travelling diet consisted of unleavened bread

Passover: a group of Jewish people gathered around a table on which a lamb is lying on a platter, woodcut from *Passional* (1552).

and roast lamb. In fact, the Bible states that there were 600,000 men, their children and their flocks: potentially millions of sheep and a very steady supply of lamb, milk and wool.

Jewish people today remember the Exodus story with the holiday of Passover. An important part of the celebration is the Seder, a ritual dinner. At these meals, a Seder plate with foods vital to the Exodus story is placed at the centre of the table. One common item is a burned lamb shank bone known as *zeroah*; while it is there to recall lamb's ritual role, it is not unwise to think of it as a reminder of what was eaten by those ancient Israelites.

The ceremonial sacrifice, and then eating, of lambs goes back to the days of ancient Babylon. In that culture, kings and gods were considered to be equivalent, so if meat was slaughtered for the gods and eaten by the king, it was the same thing. In addition, it appears that some of the slaughtered lamb meat went to the temple staff as part of their pay. It was a handy combination of worship and tithing in a world with more sheep than cash.

After the building of the Second Temple in Jerusalem around 516 BCE, Passover celebrations consisted first of a solemn service and then the carrying home of pieces of the sacrificed Passover lambs, to roast on outdoor grills. This made their celebration public and was an early expression of the now classic Passover invitation: 'Let all those who are hungry enter and eat thereof.'

With a Bible filled with lamb symbolism, it is no surprise that the main dish on one of the holiest days of the Christian calendar is often lamb. Early Christians would fast during Lent, the days before Easter, and break the fast with a meal of lamb. The lamb was a symbol both of Christ and his sacrifice and of the coming of spring. In fact, by the tenth century, the pope's Easter dinner always included a whole roast lamb.

The brass Agnus Dei (Lamb of God) from the front of the altar, Cathedral of the Assumption, Louisville, Kentucky.

Illuminated letter containing a miniature of St Agnes with a lamb, from a German choir book, 15th century.

William Blake, *Songs of Innocence and Experience* – 'The Lamb' (1789).

'St John the Baptist in the Desert', from the Limbourg Brothers' *The Belles Heures of Jean de France, Duc de Berry, c.* 1404–8.

However, it should be noted that the classic Italian Easter dish of lamb and artichokes is a classic Italian Passover dish too.

In China, half a world away, lamb was viewed with suspicion. Although sheep had been farmed and lamb eaten there since 4000 BCE, commentators of the time complained about its strong odour and pungent flavour, something that was not spoken of anywhere else during that era. This brings up at least one serious question: were the Chinese authors talking about the same animal? A quick look in a modern Chinese dictionary shows that the words for 'goat' and 'lamb' are very similar. Indeed, 'goat' can be written as 'mountain lamb'. So it could well be that they were actually objecting to goat meat.

Sheep were still raised and lamb eaten, however. Farmers saw them as a useful adjunct to pork, China's first domesticated meat animal. By the time of the Song dynasty (960–1279 CE), lamb was one of the three most commonly eaten meats, along with goat and pork. And soon after, when Kublai Khan came to China from Mongolia and founded

A bowl of Xinjiang lamb rice.

the Yuan dynasty, sheep took centre stage as the country's most important livestock. In addition, during his travels in China, Marco Polo (1254–1324) saw lambs being slaughtered in markets and described the meat as being for 'rich men and great lords'. He also said that boiled mutton was a staple food in the north of the country.

Those of less noble birth could eat rich soups made with blood and offal – an early example of a bias against organ meats. These were not the refined dishes of the wealthy, but substantial all the same. This was an era when lamb or mutton was eaten frequently by people in every walk of life and flocks of sheep were mentioned in poetry. Indeed, the Chinese saw meat animals as part of nature and celebrated it as they would the changing of the seasons, the landscape or other natural phenomena.

The Song dynasty saw another culinary 'first': the development of regional restaurants. In the city of Hangzhou, there were places that served the foods of the south, Sichuan, and the north. Of course, northern cooking included even more lamb and increased its popularity. Song-era Hangzhou was also home to many foreigners, especially Arab traders. If they had their own restaurants, those too would have offered lamb.

Hangzhou certainly already had what we would call 'fine dining' restaurants, and a menu item that translates as 'milk-steamed lamb' sounds intriguing. In addition, lamb shanks were not only on restaurant menus but were offered by street vendors, probably braised in large batches. Needless to say, there were also shops that offered lamb-filled dumplings. When Marco Polo described Hangzhou as the greatest city in the world, food was an important part of what he meant, and there, lamb was a very important ingredient. What we do not know, however, is whether the meats described as 'mutton' and 'lamb' in books of the era correspond to today's

Two raw lamb shanks.

definitions. Indeed, there are hints that 'lamb' meant newborn sheep and 'mutton' anything older.

In the tomb of a Chinese noblewoman dating from the second century BCE, a wide variety of foods were buried, including lamb. And not only were there piles of ingredients, but the tomb also contained bamboo slips with recipes – including one for a lamb and turnip stew – written on them. Other recipes called for the lamb flank and stomach.

Then – as now – the popularity of lamb, thought of as a typically northern ingredient by most Chinese people, spread to Beijing, where the nation's greatest chefs created new recipes from it. Cumin lamb now is a favourite recipe from Uighur cuisine, with thin strips of lamb meat stir-fried with cumin and chillies, the favourite spices of the region.

The Sinologist Herbert Franke has translated this lamb recipe from Manchuria:

Steamed Mutton Mei-Po

Take a whole sheep, scald and clean, and remove head, feet, intestines, etc., cut up into manageable pieces. Prepare small specimens of earth-pepper with wine and vinegar, pour over the meat and let soak for two hours or more. Put into empty metal pot, build a fire with fuel-wood sticks and seal the lid with clay. Light the fire but let it not come too close. Wait until well-cooked. To be served in bowls with original juice separately.

One cannot help but wonder if lamb was meant here rather than mutton: on a practical level, one would need a huge pot to hold an entire adult sheep, and the recipe would yield more than 100 lb (45 kg) of cooked meat.

In Greece, sheep and lambs took on their fullest roles yet. They were raised for their meat, milk, fleece, skin and horns. As anybody who eats Greek cuisine today can tell you, lamb has always been a staple of the country. During Greece's classical period, most people were living off the land, and the land was not the best for growing: conditions were hot and dry and the country was often in drought. Sheep, of course, did their usual fine job of converting sparse grass into a panoply of products that people could appreciate. With flavourings like olives, honey, wine, fish sauce, pine nuts and vinegar, along with herbs including coriander, oregano, dill, parsley and mint, Greek chefs were able to create sophisticated dishes for a wealthy upper class.

At the lower end of the economic spectrum, the poor ate far less meat; their lives were devoted to growing grain and vegetables. Lamb was not the only farm animal, though: sheep were joined by pigs, rabbits and birds of all sorts, including chickens and geese. It should be noted here that the Greeks did not take animal slaughter lightly. When it was done, it

Jason brings Pelias the Golden Fleece and a winged victory prepares to crown him with a wreath, from an Apulian red-figure calyx crater, *c.* 300–240 BC.

was always treated as a sacrifice to the gods, accompanied by prayer and ritual.

Greek farmers did not just raise sheep for their lambs, however. They were also avid cheese and yogurt makers and found sheep to be excellent milk producers. Both hard and soft cheeses were made, and today one can find Greek sheep's milk feta in markets all over the world. The Greeks were also among the world's earliest sausage eaters. By stuffing minced meat scraps, salt and seasonings into lamb intestines or stomachs, they discovered both a new way to enjoy lamb and a superb method for preserving food.

The ancient Romans ate their share of lamb too. The cookery collection known as *Apicius* or *De re coquinaria*, dating from the fourth to the fifth century CE, contains numerous meat recipes, including at least eight featuring lamb, such as lamb cooked in a cumin-seasoned broth that strongly resembles the Larsa 'boullion', and lamb stewed in wine, onions and (black) pepper. Do not think these dishes were just meat and spices thrown in a pot together: they display serious technique, including parboiling and thickening with roux.

Grilling and roasting were also found in those Roman recipes. In one dish, the lamb is first braised in broth and oil, marinated and then finished on the grill, and served with a gravy made from the marinade. Even lamb roasted over an open fire was seasoned with pepper, ginger and herbs.

The most elaborate of all the *Apicius* lamb dishes was one of stuffed lamb, in which a baby lamb is deboned through its throat so that the meat remains intact and is then cooked with seasonings in a technique similar to the French galantine, in which the meat is poached and set in aspic. A variation of this recipe includes crushed dates. Clearly, the Romans used methods that we would consider highly professional by today's standards.

By 3000 BCE, agriculture had spread to the Indian sub-continent, and with it went sheep and lamb. The biggest impact agriculture had on India was a sharp reduction in meat eating. For the first time in history, humans could grow enough plant-based foods to sustain themselves without the need for flesh. That did not stop Indian farmers from raising sheep or eating lamb, however. The *Grihya Sutras*, or 'domestic sutras', sacred Hindu texts written around 500 BCE, tell us: 'Hither are called the cows; hither are called goats and sheep; and the sweet essence of food is called hither to our house.'

Little is said in early Indian writings about lamb specifically; however, we can find an interesting clue in the diary of a fourteenth-century Arab visitor, who wrote that at a dinner he attended, each person was served between one-sixth and one-quarter of a sheep. In other words, they were eating either lamb or preposterously huge portions.

The Mughals created an entire cuisine by combining the stewed dishes and sauces they found in India with a range of new techniques. Lamb, one of their favourite meats, was

Lamb dopiaza cooking in a home kitchen.

centre stage. There were skewered *shami* and *seekh* kebabs of minced meat, *boti* kebabs of lamb pieces, *keema matar*, a curry made with minced lamb and peas, and *pasanda*, a creamy curry.

In awe of its quality, the sixteenth-century Portuguese explorer Domingo Paes described finding mutton in an Indian market that was 'so clean and fat that it looked like pork'. With that, let us take a moment to imagine how excitedly the lamb-loving British reacted when they saw those same butchers a few hundred years later.

The Islamic world also embraced the eating of lamb. Centuries after Larsa and Babylon, civilization continued to thrive in what is now Iraq. The upper classes in Baghdad were cooking lamb with a remarkable variety of flavours. A dish known as *ibrahimiya* was made with lamb, almonds, grapes, coriander, ginger and cinnamon; variations on the dish include the addition of cheese and cumin. The Iranian populace were also great lovers of meatballs – made with minced lamb, of

Kibbeh.

course. There was no shortage of technique in their cooking, either; *kurdiya*, or 'Kurdish' lamb, consisted of lamb that was first boiled whole in spiced water, then deboned, seasoned with a bit of the boiling liquid, coriander, cumin, pepper and cinnamon, and slowly poached in hot sesame oil. It was also common to stew lamb with chickpeas, as it is today.

The Egyptians had not stopped eating lamb. By the time the Islamic era began in the sixth century CE, the city of Cairo was so densely crowded that it was difficult for most people to light cooking fires at home. Instead, people bought their food already cooked. A favourite dish was spit-roasted lamb. This delicious ready-prepared meal helped to make Cairo the culinary capital of the Arab world. The legendary Persian queen Scheherazade, narrator of the *Arabian Nights*, tells of a merchant who made roast lamb for his lover. This did not mean that he actually cooked it himself – it would have been a takeaway.

The cooks in ancient Egypt had an interesting way of determining the doneness of meat: they would weigh it both before and after cooking. If it lost one-third of its weight, it was cooked; otherwise, it was too rare. This lost weight was not wasted, since the meat drippings were collected and sold too.

Lamb was not just spit-roasted in medieval Cairo. It was cooked in a tandoor, a round clay oven, and served with rice. The shredded meat and grain stew known as *harisa* (not to be confused with the North African spicy condiment *harissa*) was often made with lamb, but could just as well have contained mutton, water buffalo or beef. Lamb sausages were also eaten, as was lamb breast stuffed with nuts and spices, and lamb-filled pastries similar to today's samosas. Indeed, the makers of lamb sausages aroused the sort of suspicion they always seem to, and were accused of adding water, offal, beef or even camel meat to their products instead of lamb. It is said

A Muslim cooks lamb meat on Eid al-Adha, 2008. The festival is celebrated by sacrificing a lamb or other animal and distributing the meat to relatives, friends and the poor.

that markets required their sausage makers to be located close to the inspector's offices so that a watchful eye could be kept on them.

In the Islamic world, though, lamb was more than just a meat: it was an important symbol of faith. During Eid al-Adha, the Festival of Sacrifice, worshippers slaughter a farm animal, often a lamb, in remembrance of Abraham's near-sacrifice of his own son. None of the resulting meat goes to waste and one-third is given to the poor and needy.

For Muslims, childbirth is a time for both sacrifice and eating of lamb. The ceremony known as *Aqiqah* (see chapter Five) announces the birth and naming of a baby. Traditionally, two lambs are slaughtered for a boy and one for a girl. This creates a solemn occasion when the animals are sacrificed, a happy celebration when some of the meat is shared with friends, and a charitable act, with a portion of the meat being given to the poor.

The Greeks might have been the first sausage makers, but the Celts made a lamb sausage of a different sort by grinding organ meats, stuffing them into a lamb or sheep's stomach and hanging it over their household fires to cook, dry and cure. This dish, which came to be known as haggis, is still eaten frequently in Scotland and northern England today. There, the locals will often compare the best haggis to French pâté and the more typical mass-produced product to . . . well . . . sheep guts.

South of Scotland, the Anglo-Saxons were also big sheep farmers and lamb eaters. In medieval England, sheep were more than half the livestock kept, and lamb bones are a common find at archaeological digs. One can imagine that a hearty lamb stew would be a perfect meal for workers in one of the era's most important industries: wool.

Haggis, the Scottish classic, cooked for a Burns Night dinner.

The Ottoman rise to power and the resulting wealth that flowed into Istanbul inspired a whole new cuisine. A cookbook manuscript known in English as *The Description of Familiar Foods* from the Topkapi Palace in Istanbul and thought to date from the fourteenth century not only offers some delicious-sounding lamb and mutton dishes, but shows us an early use of what we would now call a tandoor, tandoori or *tannur* oven. This recipe calls for first poaching the lamb meat in a seasoned liquid, then covering the meat with chickpeas and walnut paste and finally cooking the meat in the oven. The seasonings used were even more ambitious, including soy sauce and carob syrup.

It is hard for us today to imagine the wild, forested Europe of the Dark Ages. Villages – often nothing more than a small group of farmers' huts surrounding a protecting castle – were islands of habitation in a sea of dense forest. In these villages, sheep continued to do their job as producers of lambs, wool and that whole constellation of by-products that they excelled in.

In the fourteenth century, cookbooks began to show up in Europe. *Le Viandier de Taillevent* was the first to detail classic French technique. Its chapter on roast meats suggests parboiling whole lambs (they must have had huge pots in those days!) and then roasting them on a spit. This meat is served with *cameline* sauce, a mixture of spices including ginger, cinnamon and mace that to our modern ears does not sound very French at all. Yet, just over a century later, a Venetian recipe for roast mutton called for a range of ingredients instantly recognizable to anybody today as Italian, including a rub of garlic, grated cheese and fennel.

One item you would never expect to see on a French royal table was meatballs, yet *Le Menagier*, a French household manual with recipes, offered '*Pommeaulx*', 'little apples' made from minced lamb, pork, herbs and spices. Take the ginger and cloves off the spice list and you have something not all that different from a meatball eaten in southern Italy 300 or 400 years later. And if meatballs are not enough, we also find a recipe for what amounts to a lamb meatloaf, filled with cheese, parsley, hyssop, sage, egg and saffron.

Sheep thrive in the chilly, damp climate of the British Isles. There, the earliest cookbook in the English language, *The Forme of Cury* from the late fourteenth century, offered a lamb recipe including almonds and cinnamon that seems straight out of the Middle East.

By the time the empires of the Ottomans and Mughals were peaking and the Renaissance had changed Europe, a new group of people were starting to emerge around the world: the working class. They did not own land, nor did they work it. Instead, they laboured in factories, shops and services. Though they did not raise any sheep, they were consumers of every product the animal produced: wearing its wool, drinking its milk and of course eating lamb.

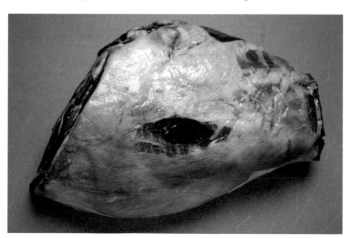

Raw leg of mutton as it came from the butcher.

Illuminated page depicting a young man roasting the Passover lamb, from the Barcelona Haggadah, *c.* 1340.

A thousand years after Apicius, Italians were still cooking his recipes. Terence Scully's translation of *Cuoco Napoletano*, by an anonymous fifteenth-century Italian master cook, includes many recipes that called for mutton, but even back then, Italians were describing the meat of sheep differently. As we will see, their 'mutton' might actually have been a young lamb in many other places. The recipes use it in ways that recall those in *Apicius*: one used minced lamb or mutton along with salted pork, eggs and 'good spices' as a stuffing for a ram's shoulder – that is, the meat of a smaller sheep stuffed into the meat of a larger one.

It was the same in Spain. The Romans brought their cuisine with them, and the Spanish traditions of eating bread, cheese, olives and wine all have their roots in the ancient Roman era. It was in Spain that the Jewish Sabbath dish of *adafina* has its roots. This stew of lamb, onions and chickpeas seems superficially similar to other traditional Spanish stews like the slow-cooked meat and bean stew *olla podrida* (a favourite of

Sancho Panza in *Don Quixote*), but in order to comply with kosher laws, olive oil was substituted for the traditional lard and lamb for pork.

You may think of the Mediterranean diet as a new phenomenon, but German cookbooks were advocating a diet that included lamb, wine and olive oil as early as the sixteenth century. Like the rest of Europe, Germans were already big lamb eaters.

Medieval cooks may have worked in a land often wracked by famine, but they worked in large quantities. Recipes often called for half or even a whole lamb, and household diaries spoke of hundreds of lambs being slaughtered for a kitchen in a matter of months. These chefs were not cooking for a single nuclear family; instead, they were acting as commissaries for the vast staffs and armies that were based in castles or manor houses. The St John's Commendam in Haarlem, Netherlands, has left us copies of its meal plans from the 1570s. The Easter Eve dinner they served included among other meats 'one quarter lamb' and two eggs 'for each lord'. So not only did kitchens of the day serve large groups, but each lord got a large serving, too.

Those of us who were not lords had an occasional serving of meat, probably preserved by salting and then cooked by boiling. And for some, boiled salted mutton was the only meat dish they knew. It would be a few more centuries before Europe bothered to set down what those who were not of the upper classes ate. And often enough, it turns out, that would be lamb.

3
Everybody's Eating Lamb

By the European Renaissance, people around the world were writing down recipes regularly; first, the food of kings and their palaces, then cookbooks started appearing for middle-class housewives, and next, social reformers wrote down the diet of the poor. Finally, explorers began setting down even the most exotic (to them) of dishes. This gives us the chance to take a proper look at how people around the world made lamb part of their daily diets.

Imagine yourself in rural Europe 200 years ago. Travel is slow; railways have not yet been built and the closest thing to an express route is a canal. Large tracts of what was once forest have been cleared for agriculture and you see sheep grazing everywhere. Towns have pretty much exploded and many are well on their way to becoming full-fledged cities. Instead of a weekly market and a single tavern, the streets are now filled with shops. Every village has its butcher and they all offer lamb. While they certainly prize them, people do not eat only the chops; every part of the animal, from the shanks to the brains, is consumed. For the shoppers who can afford it, lamb is the meat of choice. For those who are a bit less well-off, lamb's older cousin, mutton, has to do.

Another change is the age at which sheep and lambs were butchered. Back at Larsa, domestic sheep were slaughtered for food at the age of one year. Since then, that has pretty much been the definition of 'lamb' as a food. But it is in Europe at this point that things start to change. Italians begin describing lamb as the meat from animals only a few months old, and cuts of meat that are translated into English as 'mutton' are from animals that would be called 'lamb' in other places.

At the beginning of the sixteenth century, Italian recipes were not all that different from those we might have seen

Jean-Siméon Chardin, *Still-life with Leg of Lamb*, 1730.

Jan Van Eyck, *Adoration of the Lamb*, from the Ghent Altarpiece, 1430–32.

anywhere else in Europe. There were the same combinations of sweet and sour and the emphasis on exotic spices that almost could be described as typical. The Renaissance begat wealthy business families who could afford to eat like kings and were ready to pay for the privilege. This was the beginning of Italian food as we know it today.

Lamb is likely to have been the original meat filling for ravioli. *Agnolotti*, a form of filled pasta popular in Italy's Piedmont region, clearly has the Italian word for lamb, *agnello*, as its root. Even if that is not the case, lamb has been a popular meat in Italy since Roman times and has always served as a filling for stuffed pastas.

We almost never see mutton mentioned in works on Italian cuisine. Even though Italy was (and remains) a major producer of wool and sheep's cheese, the nation's food historians never seem to mention what happened to the animals after they stopped producing wool and/or milk. It is highly unlikely that they received formal burials or became pet food. Italians rarely prepared mutton as northern Europeans knew it. Instead the meat was turned into cured *salumi*. This was not only a way of making the animals more delicious, but the most practical method of preservation in the days before the chest freezer.

While many of the ingredients that we think of as Italian today, such as tomatoes and polenta, had not yet been brought over from the New World, lamb was there and being eaten. The raising of sheep for milk and cheese created a huge surplus of male newborns – a ready supply of meat. Because they were born in the spring, this created a whole category of dishes such as spring lamb paired with artichokes – a vegetable symbolic of the season.

Before there was what we would now call 'peasant cuisine', the homes of the poor had just one pot, the *paiuolo*, or cauldron.

Either hung by chains or sat on an iron tripod, it was set over the coals – the very same that roasted chestnuts, beetroots and potatoes. It was here that Italians first created modern dishes based on lamb and mutton.

Cristoforo di Messisbugo, a court cook in Ferrara, northern Italy, wrote in his book *Banchetti* (Banquets, published posthumously in 1549) that he served roasted breast of lamb. He also said that lamb was part of any well-stocked pantry. A hundred years later, Antonio Latini wrote *Lo scallo alla moderna* (The Modern Steward), a sort of guidebook to the best food products of the Kingdom of Naples, and mentioned that the area around Bari was famed for its lamb and mutton.

It was not long after Messisbugo's time that the whole range of New World ingredients started making their way into recipes in Europe. Dishes you would expect to find in Italy today – lamb braised in tomato sauce or on a bed of polenta – became possible as these New World ingredients were gradually accepted.

Lamb dishes were found all over Italy. The Piedmontese boiled lamb neck, chopped the meat up into a fine paste, then stuffed it into ravioli. These were served in a soup made with the broth from the boiled meat. In Naples, almost 950 km (600 miles) to the south, cooks were using the same broth, but in a soup with courgette (zucchini), Parmesan cheese and stale bread.

Those familiar with Tuscany's love of organ meats (often referred to as the 'fifth quarter' of a butchered animal) will enjoy a letter of 1694 from the writer Lorenzo Magalotti, in which he asks a 'sheperdess' to 'relieve his hunger by frying in lard a nice panful of [lamb] testicles'. People often argue that organ meats were eaten because meat was so expensive that none of it could go to waste, but Magalotti was not asking for scraps here. Lamb testicles were his first choice.

Fried lamb's testicles.

Domestic sheep were originally brought to North America by the Spanish in the early seventeenth century. Soon after, the Navajo Nation was the first on the continent fully to embrace the animal. Within a century, the Navajo had created their own unique breed, the Churro. Long and lean with a thick and distinctive wool, Churros were perfect for the high desert environment.

Navajo tradition tells us that even before the Spanish first brought domestic sheep to the Americas, they were in the people's genetic memory; that is to say, sheep and shepherding are an intrinsic component of who the Navajo are and how they view themselves. They are there as raisers of sheep and the sheep are there to provide them with everything from sustenance to self-expression.

A Native American (Navajo) woman sits at a loom and weaves,
c. 1904–32.

Compared to the animals being raised in the Middle
East and Europe, Churro sheep were anything but thorough-
breds. Their tough wool made the extraordinary tradition
of Navajo weaving possible, but the animals' narrow build
meant that eating them at the lamb stage was impractical.
This has made the Navajo Nation one of the few places in
the world that consumes mutton as a favourite meat while
rejecting lamb.

Sheep were so important to Navajo culture that the size of a family's herd was the key indicator of their wealth. No other possession counted for more. Today, Navajo people express this sentiment in the saying: 'If we take care of the sheep, the sheep will take care of us.' Newborn lambs were given to children as gifts so they could learn the art and science of herding from an early age. Historical photographs of Navajo children show them cuddling their lambs with great pride and affection.

Navajo dishes such as mutton stewed with green chillies and tomato present an interesting combination of New and Old World ingredients. We know that the meat came from Spain and the chillies from their own lands, while the tomatoes could have come from either – they were a prehistoric vegetable in Aztec country, a short way south of their current territory, and were part of the Spanish diet by the eighteenth century too.

In post-revolutionary France, it was a brief few decades from the time of bread shortages to the regular use of now-common techniques like roux-based sauces. Needless to say, lamb was an important foodstuff. Among the French royals, lamb was one of the most favoured foods, and when the French common people finally got the chance, they all wanted to try it.

Those first restaurant customers could choose *ratons du mouton*, lamb fillets stuffed with poultry and herbs, and a dish of saddle of lamb braised with bacon, bone marrow and foie gras known as *selle de mouton à la Barberine*. Named after a famous Italian family, the dish might be expected to have Italian roots, but the foie gras tells us otherwise. A recipe dating from 1746 for lamb and turnip stew shows us a simpler dish, although the lamb itself remained a luxury ingredient.

'April', from the Da Costa Hours, Belgium, *c.* 1515.

By 1820 recipes were written down that can be truly described as modern French cooking. A lamb or mutton neck served with a purée of lentils is typical of the era. Another dish, lamb chops *à la soubise*, looks modern, with chops, pieces of ham and vegetables cooked together in a pot and the chops glazed in the reduced cooking liquid at the end. Both dishes call for the lamb to be wrapped in lard, giving it an unctuousness that few would enjoy today. Most surprising perhaps is a recipe called 'Seven Hour Lamb'. It is a nineteenth-century take on the sort of long, low-temperature cooking that is very popular today, but with the grand French additions of whole truffles, *cornichons* and, of course, pork fat.

Lamb found its way into French pâtés too. One recipe called for the fillet meat of lamb chops, bacon, cayenne pepper, mace, lemon peel and breadcrumbs. This was then baked in puff pastry and sliced.

While the French had always eaten lamb and mutton, its popularity waxed and waned. In an article for the magazine *Household Words* Charles Dickens wrote:

> The desecration of French cookery reigns along the Riviera more or less. At Mentone [*sic*], where there are also many English people, the characteristic dishes of the locality are disappearing fast. Thirty years ago, pollenta [*sic*] was eaten in every household, and stockfish, with tomatoes and potatoes, was a general favourite. Now these things exist no longer in the flourishing town on the borders of Italy; mutton cutlets, legs of mutton, and joints of beef are more favoured.

In Britain, cookery books were showing up with increasing frequency. In *The Art of Cookery Refin'd and Augmented, Containing an Abstract of some Rare and Rich Unpublished Receipts*

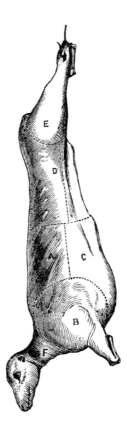

Engraving of a lamb carcass from Mrs Beeton's *The Book of Household Management* (1863).

of Cookery (1654) by Joseph Cooper, we find recipes for stewed loin of lamb, boiled joint of lamb, a hash of lamb and even haggis (called 'Haggus-puddings' by Cooper). Described as 'chiefe cook to the late king', Cooper clearly intended his book for the professional kitchens of its time and the homes of the wealthy.

Looking at these old books, we see more than just recipes. In 1584, at a time when other British authors were suggesting that lamb could be 'phlegmatic', the physician Thomas Cogan wrote: 'it is seldom seene that any man hath taken harme by eating raw mutton, so light and wholesome it is in digestion' – a statement that might make you ask whether he was talking about the leaner, more tender and delicately flavoured meat of the lamb instead. Indeed, half a century later, the British journalist Thomas Moffat described lamb as 'of all others our best nourishment': a resounding endorsement.

Seventeenth-century Dutch recipes seem to hark back to the Middle Ages in interesting ways. The dish 'Whole Haunch of Mutton in the English Manner with a Sauce' contained the butter one would expect from a good English sauce, and capers, an exotic ingredient for both the British and the Dutch. A dish then called *hutspot* was a stewed whole haunch of sheep with a butter and artichoke sauce. There was also a variation called a Spanish *hutspot*, with small bits of stewed mutton under an egg yolk sauce that is almost like zabaglione. In a recipe that seems to cover all bases, they stewed capon, mutton, beef, pork, duck and sausages together with ginger and savoy cabbage. There is no mention of how many eaters this dish would serve.

Even though the Dutch raised their sheep for wool and kept most of them – male or female – until maturity, lamb still showed up in the occasional recipe. In a Dutch version of *olipodrigo*, the Spanish meat and bean stew, we see a 'good' version with mutton and a more 'sumptuous' one using lamb. This latter recipe really is sumptuous – not only does it have lamb, capon, veal and beef, but it contains balls of minced ham, sweetbreads and marrow bones and is seasoned with pepper and mace. The vegetables served with it include chestnuts, asparagus and artichokes.

Which came first: the roast, or the fork to eat it with? You might think that before the British started using forks regularly, they would have preferred dishes that were easy to eat with a knife alone or perhaps spooned on a trencher

Cawl, the classic Welsh lamb stew.

(a piece of bread that doubled as a plate). Yet we see mentions of whole legs of lamb – or even entire lambs – on the menu before this was the case. Were they like the refined diners in India of today who eat with their hands without making the slightest bit of mess?

A few years ago, I chatted with a man in a Scottish small-town pub who flatly refused to eat lamb. It was clear that he was not a vegetarian; instead, he was still bitter about the Highland Clearances, the forced removal in the eighteenth and nineteenth centuries of vast numbers of tenant farmers to make way for sheep. With almost nobody farming – or even living – on the land, it was possible to create vast flocks of sheep and have a supply of lamb and wool that could feed the newly industrialized cities.

Those farmers became the employees of Britain's rapidly expanding industrial sector, the residents of its new colonies and, it was hoped, lamb eaters. In order to find out how they were eating it, we can turn to the seminal cookbook *The Art of Cookery Made Plain and Easy* (1747), written by Hannah Glasse. She begins with suggestions for shopping, urging the reader to 'mind the neck-vein; if it be an azure blue it is new and good, but if greenish or yellowish, it is near tainting, if not tainted already.' Mrs Glasse also recommends sniffing beneath the kidneys, really helping to paint a picture of what a butcher's shop of the time was like.

Given the grand British tradition of making meat pies, you might expect a savoury lamb pie from Glasse, but she offers a

Seasoned leg of mutton ready for cooking.

recipe for a sweet pie with lamb, raisins, currants, sugar and candied citrus peel. This was to be served with a sauce made from white wine and egg yolks.

Mrs Glasse offered other lamb dishes, too. She cooked them in ale, wine, capers and nutmeg with a method described as 'frying' – even though it seems more like braising to modern eyes. She also made a 'ragoo' out of lamb, bacon, herbs and oysters, and suggested more than one way of cooking a whole lamb's head. Not only did people eat a huge amount of lamb, but the entire animal was destined for the table – they did not just eat the chops and turn the rest to compost.

A menu from The Queen's Hotel in Manchester dated 25 January 1865 offers 'Lamb Cutlets aux Petits Pois' as a starter, and a saddle of mutton under a category of dishes called *relevés* – an extra meat course, part of the huge meals served up at the time. On another menu from a year later from the same hotel, one finds mutton cutlets offered as well. As one of the world's leading wool producers, Britain had an awful lot of mutton to consume.

Just sixteen years after Henry Hudson's first visit to New York Harbor in 1609, sheep were brought from the Netherlands to New York City, where they immediately started producing the meat and fibre they were known for. By the 1650s, market prices were established for both the buying and selling of animals and their slaughter. One commenter of the era wrote: 'I have seen mutton so exceedingly fat there, that it was too luscious and offensive.' People ate it, though, and a diary entry of 1704 lists 'leg of mutton and pickles' as an extravagant meal.

Americans bred more sheep after the Stamp Act was introduced in 1765, as a way of avoiding the tax on imported wool. It was hoped that this would increase wool production, but it did not work that way. Instead, most of the animals were slaughtered at a young age and consumed as lamb, with only a small few left alive for breeding. Lamb meat was just too popular.

In the Americas, a remarkable exchange was taking place. The Spanish brought in domesticated sheep and the indigenous peoples taught them a wonderful new cooking technique. The first word used to describe it was *barbacoa*. This was a Spanish rendering of a Taíno word for a sort of smoking-cooking set-up and the meats that came out of it. By 1800 English-speakers were using the word 'barbecue' to describe meats prepared this way, and whole sheep or lambs were a commonly barbecued item. The word *barbacoa* persists to this day in Latin America, where it continues to describe a meal often made with a whole lamb. *Appletons' Guide to Mexico* (1884) tells us that 'Beef and mutton, as well as poultry, are generally to be had at breakfast and dinner in the *fondas* (as simple, local restaurants are often called) throughout the Republic', while lamb is barely mentioned.

Barbacoa was not the only south-of-the-border dish containing lamb. The meat was making its way into soups and stews, too, in all cases going perfectly with corn tortillas, the region's staple. Indeed, stewing was such a common technique that we can find regional recipes for stewed lamb chops – a cut that is considered perfect for grilling or frying anywhere else. *Mixiotes de carnero*, lamb steamed in *maguey* (agave) leaves and avocado leaves, and *carnero con ajo*, a roast mutton leg larded with garlic, were also found.

Food in nineteenth-century North America was very similar to British fare, with a few Dutch and native dishes mixed in. *Martha Washington's Booke of Cookery* offers several notable dishes including a fricassee of lamb, and a leg of lamb stuffed with – among other items – anchovies, capers and lemon peel. Martha offered far more recipes for mutton.

Bernhard Plockhorst, *The Good Shepherd*, late 19th century.

A bowl of grilled lamb's kidneys.

Besides the usual roasts, there was a free-form pie (which she called a 'pasty') filled with mutton and sheep's blood, a pie of sheep's tongue and kidney, and a mention of lamb 'stones' – the testicles that our Italian friend also craved (see pp. 50–51).

By the middle of the nineteenth century, things began to change. As North America became a melting pot of cultures, people began eating lamb and mutton in entirely different ways. Cookbooks of the time offer recipes for everything from lamb chop suey to Spanish lamb hash. For example, in the book *German National Cookery for American Kitchens* (1904) by Henriette Davidis, we find fifteen mutton recipes and five more for lamb. They include a very Scottish-sounding mutton broth with barley, made German with the addition of potato dumplings; a stew of mutton with turnips; and the most curious 'lamb chops for invalids'. This turns out to be well-trimmed lamb chops, larded then fried in butter, and then braised in a Madeira-thickened meat broth. Davidis also suggests that 'Roasts . . . mutton or lamb, should be reckoned at 1 pound (including the bones) for each person' – a good indicator of portion sizes at the time.

Thriving cities of the Arab Mediterranean, such as Istanbul and Cairo, continued to be major centres for what were becoming classic lamb dishes. Modern readers of *Bradshaw's Hand-Book to the Turkish Empire* (*c.* 1872) can see that people there were eating a diet not all that different from what we might find there today. What has changed are the attitudes. George Bradshaw recommends that travellers choose mutton over beef or pork because it is lighter, but goes on to describe skewered mutton as a 'national dish'.

Iran's national dish, *chelo* kebabs – hot-dog-shaped patties of minced lamb grilled and served with rice – is similar to those Turkish dishes in ingredients and cooking method. Indeed, it seems that grilling minced lamb is more than just a regional tradition. In fact, it is something that is seen up and down the route of the Silk Road, the great trade route between China and Europe. *Chelo* kebabs were also the first street foods in Iran, and then among the first local foods to be served when sit-down restaurants in the country started offering Iranian dishes along with European ones at the beginning of the twentieth century.

One can go a long way east on the Silk Road and still find kebabs of this type – from the Middle East through Samarkand in Uzbekistan all the way to Xi'an in central China. There one can find lamb and mutton skewered and roasted over charcoal grills, not all that different from the street foods of Turkey and Greece, a third of the world away.

It is in this corner of the world – wedged between Russia and China – that the legendary fat-tailed sheep originated.

Khoresht-e aloo, an Iranian lamb stew with prunes.

Plate of the Uzbek dish *plov.*

Shepherd in Afghanistan with a fat-tailed sheep.

With up to 20 per cent of their body weight in their (obviously) very fat backsides, they produce a rich meat that people in this area treasure. Without seeing these sheep, it is hard to imagine just how big their tails are. In fact, when fattening the animals for the market, farmers will rig carts to support them and the weight of their tails. Visitors to the region will find not only lamb kebabs and lamb-filled dumplings but also dishes such as rice pilaf cooked with 'fatty lamb', or simply lamb fat, from those big tails.

This is not the only culinary use of lamb fat. In Central Asia, it is used in the same way as rendered bacon, goose or chicken fat for frying, baking or just as a butter-like spread. The ultimate form, though, is the lamb-fat kebabs: skewered chunks of lamb fat alternated with pieces of onion and bell pepper. As the fat roasts over the coals it fries the neighbouring vegetables, giving them a unique, double-cooked flavour.

All these seemingly exotic kebabs bring us to an important point in time: the beginning of what we would call the modern era. Yes, kebabs were eaten in faraway places long ago, and they are also eaten almost everywhere in the world today.

4
Lamb Today

What has happened to the lamb, the first farm animal? Today, lamb is the most widely consumed meat in the Middle East and south Asia, and while it is not as popular as it once was in Europe and North America, it is making a comeback. Let us take a look at the ways in which people across the world cook and eat lamb today.

Though you might be amazed to learn that anybody in the United States eats mutton at all, New York City has a restaurant that is famous for serving it: Keens Steakhouse. Keens works hard to portray itself as an eatery from another era. A mutton chop is on the menu, and its role is to remind diners of the great meat restaurants of New York City's past.

With that in mind, I paid Keens a visit. Alone and on a lunch break, I was not ready for the suit-filled dining room. The bar turned out to be fine, though, and the sight of at least a few other people working on their chops was encouraging. Soon, the mutton was placed in front of me. There was a hunk of sheep flesh with a flawless steakhouse char and two truncated rib bones. These were either the smallest mutton chops or the largest lamb chops I'd ever seen. It gave new meaning to the phrase 'mystery meat'. This was a double-thick chop from a teenage animal (a 'hogget' or 'yearling' in sheep-farmer

Sheep at Ewetopia, a small farm in Vermont.

jargon). Keens is rightly revered as New York's temple of sheep meat.

Except for this single restaurant, the town of Owensboro, Kentucky, and the Navajo Nation in Arizona, mutton is almost impossible to find in America. In Britain, it's another story entirely. There, a roast mutton leg or shoulder shows up on menus fairly often. And in the rest of the modern world, lamb is the sheep meat of choice.

Lamb rarely – if ever – takes centre stage in American home cooking today. There is leg of lamb as a traditional dish for Easter and Passover, but little else. It has not always been this way. In the early twentieth century, lamb was everywhere: on the menus at important banquets, lunch counters and every sort of place in between.

From Turkey to Germany

Let's face it, 1938 was not the best year for a teenager from Turkey to pack up and move to Germany. Mahmut Aygun did just that, though. Aygun thought that no matter which way the winds of war blew, a snack shop – especially one that sold those Turkish meat skewers called 'kebabs' – would be in demand. Throughout the 1960s, he served his kebabs the traditional way: on a bed of rice with a vegetable side. This was fine when most people came to places like his for a sit-down meal, but far less satisfactory when customers wanted something to take away. Aygun needed something both inexpensive

Slicing a giant doner kebab.

and portable, a combination of classic Turkish ingredients that a person could buy, walk away with and consume without the trappings of a sit-down restaurant – even if they were dead drunk. On 2 March 1971, from his shop in Berlin, he began selling his answer: the doner kebab. It was (and still is) slices of minced lamb (and, all too often, other meats), cooked on a vertical spit and served in the pocket of a traditional Middle Eastern pitta bread.

Even though the kebab was a great success in this simple form, Aygun also went on to create the yogurt sauce that many people associate with doner kebabs today. Aygun's creation quickly became northern Europe's go-to portable snack, as ubiquitous as Mexico's taco and Italy's pizza and just as global. It was the world's oldest meat made modern.

That vertical spit of roasting minced lamb shows up in many other places too. Mexico might not have been receptive to pitta bread, but, brought over by Lebanese immigrants and renamed *al pastor*, our sliced lamb suddenly found itself under a spicy sauce, wrapped in a taco and served with a wedge of lime.

Kebabs have a longer history, of course. In earlier times, people needed a way to cook with only tiny amounts of fuel and the small fires that resulted. Cut-up bits of meat and vegetable on a stick placed directly over the coals would roast quickly and deliciously before the energy source cooled down. When cooking fuel became more abundant, kebabs remained popular, because they could be prepared one portion at a time. More than anything, this is what makes them such an ideal street food.

Today, Turkey is the lamb street- and snack-food capital of the world. Look for *uykuluk* – lamb sweetbreads grilled on skewers (my favourite). Remember, though, that these are neither bread nor sweet. Instead, they are the animal's thymus glands. *Çöp şiş* (yes . . . this means 'trash kebabs'), skewers composed of the small bits of meat left over from butchering larger cuts, are often eaten ten or fifteen at a time. And, lest you think that everything there is served on skewers, there are also *tantuni*, wrap sandwiches made from minced lamb and vegetables, and *beyran*, a spicy soup that includes lamb fat, lamb meat and rice.

In East Asia you will find 'skewer alleys', or rows of street-food vendors offering familiar and not-so-familiar items cooked kebab-style. Look for skewers of lamb seasoned in every conceivable way, along with sticks of lamb's liver, kidney, sweetbreads and testicle.

Lamb is second to pork as the meat of choice in China, but this statement does not give a realistic impression, since pork is consumed so much more widely than any other meat that it dwarfs all comparisons. People who are both street-food and lamb fanatics really must head to Xi'an city. Besides being the capital of Shaanxi Province and home to the famed Terracotta Warriors, it is lamb-eating central and home to a formidable collection of vendors; the 'Muslim Night Market' or 'Muslim Snack Street' is the favourite spot for them.

Begin with *yang rou chuan*: kebabs, of course, marinated with cumin and other spices. Then try *guan tang baozi*, soup dumplings filled with mutton and served with a dipping sauce containing Sichuan peppers. Next, grab a few *rou jia mo*, a kind of bread roll filled with minced mutton or beef. Finally, finish your meal with a lamb noodle soup such as *dao xiao mian*.

In Singapore you'll find satay, the Southeast Asian version of kebabs, made from mutton – a meat with flavours strong enough to counter the even stronger seasonings with which they are made. And in Indonesia, where kebab-like satay sticks are likewise a staple, you can also find distinctively spiced lamb soups.

Kebabs can be found on the streets of Africa, too. There you will find lamb on skewers, but with one big difference: those skewers will be deep-fried instead of grilled. South African street-food vendors sell foods with influences you might expect – such as Indian samosas, spelled *samoosa* in this part of the world, filled with minced lamb – and ones you might not expect, such as 'Gatsbys', American-style submarine sandwiches. Eaters who are adventurous and possess a sarcastic edge should grab a 'smiley' – a whole grilled sheep's head. Aficionados know that the tongue and brains will be delicious, and the eyes have their fans too. If there's somebody squeamish along for the ride, they can have the cheeks. And yes, the name 'smiley' comes from the grin that stares back at you while you eat.

In central Africa, you are just as likely to find stews as kebabs, be they the famed *tibs* of Ethiopia or curries in Tanzania. In either case, you'll find powerful flavours; chillies, curry, leafy herbs, garlic and lemon. In Ethiopia, stews are served with the country's unique flatbread, injera. When you get your spicy lamb dish *awaze tibs* and injera, you will not be offered utensils. Instead, you should tear off pieces of the crêpe-like bread and use them to scoop up, grab or wipe up the food, depending on where you are in your meal. In the rest of central Africa, look for soups and stews flavoured with peanut butter. To most of us in the West, a bowl of peanut-butter-and-lamb stew sounds pretty frightening, but one taste and you will quickly realize that you have grossly underestimated peanut butter's potential.

North Africa has many stews of its own. *Bamya*, made from lamb and okra, is an Egyptian favourite, while tagines of all kinds are popular in Morocco. Both are served with wheat-derived grains such as bulgur or couscous.

In India, McDonald's is the place to find lamb. Since cows are considered sacred by many in this country, the global

Mutton chop frying in a grill pan.

chain had to consider a substitute meat for its burgers when opening in India. Lamb was perfect: it makes a great burger and is not only accepted but enthusiastically consumed by most meat eaters. And if you're not a burger eater, you can step out on the street and get lamb kebabs – in this case marinated in Indian spices and cooked in a clay tandoori oven.

By the early twentieth century, visitors to Mexico were demanding something previous generations had tried to avoid: the native cuisine. An authentic Mexican taco consists of meat, cheese and vegetables wrapped in a soft corn tortilla. However, while foreigners almost always choose a filling of minced beef (with chicken as a very distant second), Mexicans fill theirs with all sorts of meat, including turkey, pork and, yes, mutton. Sheep meat is found as a taco filling everywhere in the country.

There is more lamb to be had in otherwise beef-crazed South America. *Seco de cordero* is Peru's lamb stew, made with potatoes and peppers. Take a close look at those mixed grills in places like Argentina and you will see a lamb chop there often enough.

Australian cuisine began with indigenous foods, but the early British colonists wanted something more familiar. It was not a big step from bringing over a few sheep to grazing large numbers of them. The facts are clear. With a population of about 23 million people and about the same number of portions of lamb meat sold each week, they're eating quite a bit of the stuff. Not enough for it to be the most popular meat (which is beef), but enough.

This has not stopped an Australian restaurant in Brooklyn, New York, from calling itself Sheep Station and putting roast leg of lamb on the menu. At home, however, Australian food reflects its history as a melting pot with British roots. As well as roast leg of lamb and shepherd's pie, thanks to its vibrant multicultural culinary scene you'll also find lamb dishes from every other corner of the planet.

A serving of braised lamb shank.

Since the 1980s, we have also seen an explosion in the number of fine-dining restaurants. In the past, a few cities, such as Paris, had a small group of eateries serving a refined and creative cuisine to the wealthiest customers. The rest of the world looked at these places with a mixture of jealousy and disdain. But, starting in the 1980s, fine dining started showing up in unexpected places, including the college town of Berkeley, California, and the pubs of rural England. Country dining in Italy and Spain, formerly thought of as the realm of small local businesses serving a few home-cooked dishes to passing salesmen and tourists, took on a whole new profile. Of course, lamb was an important ingredient – even in places where it normally was not eaten.

The Greek American chef Michael Psilakis, a familiar face to American television viewers, went so far as to call his cookbook *How to Roast a Lamb: New Greek Classic Cooking* (2009). Besides inspired versions of the classics, including 'Braised

Rack of lamb, the most elegant cut the animal offers.

Lamb Tongue with White Beans and Mushrooms' and grilled lamb chops, it includes a recipe for a whole spit-roasted lamb. Beginning with 'decapitate the lamb', Psilakis presents clear directions for this most intimidating of tasks. This is a recipe for a dish so big it calls for 2 quarts (about 2 l) of lemon juice. In his Manhattan restaurant Kefi, the menu includes Greek dishes like lamb sausage and braised lamb shanks with orzo. Psilakis made his greatest impact, however, at his short-lived restaurant Anthos in New York. There, dishes like his braised lamb and pasta casserole *pastitsio* reinvented traditional recipes – and Greek cuisine – for the modern era.

Unfortunately, lamb continues to have something of a bad reputation in parts of China. There, some pregnant women avoid lamb and mutton because they fear it will cause their child to be epileptic – a concern brought on by linguistic similarities. Indeed, the word for 'epilepsy' is sometimes written in Chinese as 'Mad Lamb Disease'. Lamb is still raised, though. In the rugged highlands they excel at converting the sparse, dry grass to succulent meat. After all, pigs, for all their virtues, cannot live on hay.

In *Pei Mei's Chinese Cook Book* (1969) many lamb recipes are offered. Some, such as 'Jellied, Stewed Mutton' – meat moulded in a sort of aspic – are virtually unknown outside China. And Pei's 'Rinsed Mutton in Chafing Pot' is what hotpots were like before modern cooks removed the organ meats from them. We can also find 'Sautéed Lamb with Spring Onion', a fairly common item on today's Chinese menus. 'Rinsed' is a pretty literal translation of what English-speakers might call 'dipping', or maybe even 'fondue' (although there certainly isn't any cheese). Commonly called 'hotpot' today, these dishes consist of a pot of heated broth placed in the centre of the table, into which diners dip thinly sliced lamb, vegetables and other items. After the meat is finished, the diners sip the

Piece of lamb being dipped in hot sauce after being cooked in a hotpot.

remaining broth, which is now deeply flavoured by the 'rinsed' lamb and vegetables.

Even the Polynesian restaurant craze that swept America during the 1960s saw lamb on menus. Ren Clark's Polynesian Village in Fort Worth, Texas, offered an Indonesian *Saugeed* Lamb Curry. I cannot help but wonder how spicy it was or if it actually bore any resemblance to Indonesian cuisine. Of course, in those days there could not have been more than a handful of Indonesians in all of North America – nobody was checking the authenticity of these dishes.

Modern mass media has created a wholly different way of disseminating recipes. All over the world, diners are visiting the restaurants and buying the products of chefs whom they have seen on television, and the dishes they offer have a strong influence on eating habits.

In her book *Feast: Food that Celebrates Life* (2004), Nigella Lawson offers Slow Cooked Lamb with Beans. She also has a recipe for Lamb Shanks with Figs and Honey, which seems to be a combination of braised lamb shanks and pumpkin pie. The legendary Two Fat Ladies did the same. On their pioneering TV show, Jennifer Paterson and Clarissa Dickson Wright, both passionate food enthusiasts and cooks, would ride around Britain on a motorcycle with sidecar looking for combinations of great cooking and traditional activities. The Two Fat Ladies were revolutionary: they went on prime-time television and told British viewers that their traditional foods and dishes were interesting, delicious and, most of all, worth cooking

Marcus Samuelsson, a Swedish chef born in Ethiopia whose interests range from the cuisine of Sweden to African spices and American soul food, used lamb for a number of dishes in his book *The Soul of a New Cuisine* (2006). In it, recipes like Berbere-Crusted Rack of Lamb and Za'atar-Roasted Leg of Lamb combine classical Continental restaurant techniques with African flavours. Samuelsson's restaurant, Red Rooster in Harlem, New York, offers a menu that consists mainly of soul food with twists that reflect his roots. The dish Lamb and Potato Hash brings the Continental influence of lamb to a traditional American hash, on perhaps the only menu on the planet that offers dishes with berbere spices from Ethiopia next to Swedish meatballs with lingonberries. The result is new, inviting and not too deeply anchored in one cuisine or another.

Lamb is no stranger to the multi-Michelin-starred French restaurants at the top of the gastronomic tree. Master chefs such as Alain Ducasse serve lamb on almost all their menus. This is French cuisine at its most elaborate and creative; no 'double-thick lamb chops' here! Instead, Ducasse offers stuffed boneless legs of lamb with truffles; spit-roasted lamb served with French artichokes; and stuffed lamb chops with summer vegetables. Compare these dishes to the kebabs you find on Turkish streets and you will find the true range of lamb represented. It is both the most informal and the most formal of ingredients. Indeed, no matter what cooks ask of it, lamb does the job.

5
Future Meat:
The Small Farm Returns

Torrey Reade's Neptune Farm is a long way down a dirt road that is in itself a long way down a narrow two-lane road. The nearest town is Salem, New Jersey – almost half an hour away by car. An urban escapee, Reade began her homestead almost 25 years ago, starting with a large vegetable crop, blueberries and a cow to supply her with milk. Soon it became obvious that berries and vegetables were going to be a tough sell, and that sheep and the lambs they produced would work brilliantly.

Today, Reade offers her meat to consumers by the whole or half animal, butchered, wrapped and ready for the freezer, and to restaurants as freshly slaughtered whole animals. Her farm has found its ideal product. I stopped by one day and spoke to her about it.

During the first season Reade was lambing, she fully expected to be celebrating the joy of new life and the appearance of spring, but instead was terrified. 'Our sheep weren't suitable for lambing, one yelled and cried and another had a breech delivery. Some lambs came out backwards and stillborn.' At this point, Reade reminded me that there is no such thing as a sheep maternity hospital. A sheep in labour might scrape at the ground for a minute or two – and there are some

The sheep of Neptune Farm.

shepherds who can recognize that moment and hustle the animal inside – but to most people, it looks as though they simply lie down and give birth.

There is a saying in the sheep-farming world: 'You either have a well sheep or a dead sheep.' I took this to mean that the animals are hardy when healthy but succumb quickly when ill. Of course, I was wrong. In fact, the problem is the cost of veterinary care. Because a visit by a large-animal veterinarian costs more than the market value of a typical sheep, there is no way to justify the expense.

This came as a shock. My idea of a rural vet was developed entirely by reading the partially autobiographical novels of James Herriot. I just couldn't imagine Herriot leaving Reade's sheep to die. In real life, though not in his stories, Dr James Alfred 'Alf' Wight – who wrote as James Herriot and practised veterinary medicine in North Yorkshire, a place where there are sheep as far as the eye can see – must have made such decisions.

One thing I couldn't help but notice is that every sheep farmer I encountered was a woman. Certainly this was not co-incidence. I asked Mary Peabody, the director of the Women's Agricultural Network at the University of Vermont, for her take on this. She explained that women made up the majority of new farmers and that women preferred to farm sheep because they are smaller and more docile than cows, and cost less both to buy and to maintain. She assured me that there were indeed men raising sheep on larger properties in the West, Australia and elsewhere.

Not all new farmers are near big cities. Earlier, we learned about the Navajo Nation and their Churro sheep. First brought over by the Spanish and seen by the Navajo as a gift of God, then slaughtered to near-extermination by American government officials trying to eradicate Navajo culture and traditions, the Churro sheep are having a resurgence. By the 1970s, there were fewer than 500 traditional Churro sheep alive

New Jersey farmer Shelly Nussbaum with one of her sheep.

in the United States (down from over 500,000 before U.S. Government intervention), and the Navajo people were in a state of crisis. No other breed of sheep was remotely as well-adapted to the unique conditions of Navajo lands in New Mexico and Arizona.

Like many people around the world, the Navajo needed the astounding range of products the sheep provided. It was not just meat and wool; there was more to this than a stew or a sweater. The unique fibre of the Churro was a key material for local weavers – the people who created the blankets and other textiles that are an important part of Navajo patrimony and are known the world over.

The Navajo people continue to eat mutton as a staple meat. The menu board at the Mitchell Butte Diner near Monument Valley, Arizona, included Roast Mutton with Green Chilli, and Mutton Stew with Cabbage; both are served with frybread (deep-fried, flat dough) or tortillas. It is the same at cafés, restaurants and even food trucks across the Navajo Nation: mutton is the meat of choice.

Today, with a population of about 5,000 animals, the Churro remains an endangered breed, but the numbers are growing, not shrinking, and breeders from as far away as Connecticut and Wisconsin are pitching in to help. Slow Food, the international local foods advocacy group, has put the Churro on its Ark of Taste – a collection of foods that are in danger of extinction.

In addition to the Navajo Churro, the Ark of Taste lists 41 sheep breeds. These range from the Bulgarian Karakachan to the Norwegian Villsau, thought to be the breed favoured by Scandinavians long before the Viking era. To my surprise, five on the list were from the Italian region of Piedmont, a place known today for its fine wine and beef. A hundred years ago, though, less beef and more wool was produced there, and as we have learned, people in those days used the sheep as a complete source of production and could not afford to keep animals for just one purpose. Towns that today are home to a few hundred retirees and foreign holidaymakers once held 1,000 or more extended families and perhaps a hundred times as many sheep. Wool, meat and hides were their main commercial connection with the outside world.

The Italian breed that has attracted the most attention, though, is the Zeri (now known as the Zerasca). Although the village of Zeri is technically in Tuscany, it is so far removed from the region's main gastronomic tourism routes that it has little impact. It seems that this is actually part of the problem: as nearby areas became more and more affluent, the smaller farmers left and took jobs in places like Florence and Pisa, while the larger and more successful ones gave up the local sheep for breeds with more commercial appeal.

By the turn of the twenty-first century, there were only a few Zerasca sheep left. Known only by the locals, these sheep had mild, tender meat, and while they produced very little milk, it was so concentrated with protein and fat that its yield for cheese was extraordinary. There were only two problems: the lack of sheep and the lack of farmers. Indeed, almost all the Zerasca sheep left were in the hands of a few women who lived in the area and had inherited bits of land. So, in 2001, they created the Consortium for the Development and Protection of the Zeri Lamb. This gave the animals a tiny bit of recognition; a recent film, *The Women of Zeri*, and several appearances at Slow Food conferences have provided badly needed publicity.

Zerasca sheep are typically 60–75 cm (24–9 inches) high at the shoulder, putting them in the middle of the sheep-size spectrum. They have long legs and necks, and small horns. It is a good thing they are as mild-mannered as they are, because the women of Zeri use those horns as handles to move the animals. Indeed, a high point in *The Women of Zeri* occurs when one of the women gently pulls a newborn lamb from its mother's womb while another holds the mother sheep by the horns.

In the end, however, the problems the women of Zeri face are the same that sheep farmers everywhere have to deal with: keeping their flocks healthy and getting them and their products to market. One of the goals of these women is to build their own slaughterhouse so that they do not have to cover the cost of transporting the animals and can have control over what happens to the carcasses. As a result they would be able to profit from animals that have reached the end of their productive lives; today, they are sold off for a few euros and nobody even asks what happens to them. With their own abattoir, they would be able to bring back yet another lost art: the making of sausages and cured meats from mutton.

It is a familiar story: tiny parcels of land, not enough money, and animal husbandry skills that have to be learned from scratch. You hear it all over North America and Europe, too. It even applies to Africa. An older woman on the land in Ethiopia might not be able to handle cattle, but can easily keep a modest flock of sheep. Though this may sound like little more than a hobby to those of us in the developed West, in Africa it can be the difference between poverty and a good life. Remember that notion of sheep as a factory? It means no less today than it did thousands of years ago. We just have to pay attention to it.

Lamb and Modern Religious Ritual

In an earlier chapter, we learned about Muslim ceremonies and celebrations that involve lamb. Let us now explore the impact they have on farmers today. As one might expect, exports from the major lamb-producing nations of Australia and New Zealand to the Middle East are strong, but so are farm-to-consumer sales in places where Muslims have not traditionally lived. Ceremonies like *Aqiqah* and the Hajj, which require the slaughter of a lamb, have motivated farmers in places that are not traditionally Muslim, such as Pennsylvania and Yorkshire, to build separate facilities for Islamic ritual slaughter.

There is a problem, though: the celebrants – those who have to slaughter the lamb – are often educated urban professionals who have not only never killed a lamb before, but have rarely even visited a farm. While this inexperience generates concern among all farmers, it especially pains those who are

Locally raised lambs for sale at the Hackettstown Livestock Auction in New Jersey.

themselves observant Muslims. Hisham Moharram is one such farmer, and, for him, being humane is not an option – it is a requirement. He told me what this means to him:

> You raise animals on an open pasture without chemicals, you give them water, you give them freedom to live and enjoy and run and be happy and in the course of doing [so] . . . when the time comes to harvest that meat, you will get a high-quality product, you'll be safe in your health, and . . . on the day of judgment you won't have to explain yourself.

These ritual needs call for tolerant supervision. First, the farmers have to inspect the tools used to make sure they are the correct ones for the job, and then they must provide qualified staff and proper instruction in the slaughtering technique.

Meanwhile, mutton seems to be holding its own. The 'locavore' local food movement has played a role, but the demand for mutton in ethnic markets has done even more. In places such as Hispanic butcher's shops and supermarkets, mutton – which had previously been nothing but a food one read about in old novels – is now a popular meat. And for those lucky enough to be near authentic restaurants serving cuisines that embrace the meat, it can be eaten cooked in traditional ways there too.

All this interest in sheep farming has created a curious new activity: mutton busting. In this rodeo event, small children ride sheep in the same way that adults ride bulls. However, sheep and bulls do not really behave in similar ways, and six-year-olds do not comport themselves in the same way as professional bull riders. Instead, the children seem to hug the sheep as they stroll rather than rush out of the gate, and are often able to stay on for quite a while. Even when the

Lamb loin chops frying in a grill pan.

children fall off, sheep – unlike bulls – will stop and wait for their riders to remount, or join their riders as they walk back to their waiting parents.

Over much of the past decade Britain has been the scene of an enthusiastic mutton renaissance. In fact, Prince Charles has launched an organization with the very name Mutton Renaissance. His campaign sets a standard for meat quality with specifications for feed, traceability, ageing and method of slaughter. In creating the organization, Prince Charles spoke of how he enjoyed mutton as a child and was saddened to have watched it vanish from British menus.

The campaign seems to be working. There has been an explosion of mutton dishes in restaurants all over Britain, and a whole group of chefs who advocate 'nose to tail eating'. For many chefs, as for Prince Charles, mutton represents a traditional pastoral Britain, where wool was an important export and there was enough mutton for everyone to eat.

While much has been said about the role of lamb in the resurgence of small farms, it has also become an engine for export income. Australia and New Zealand, both sparsely populated and perfectly suited to lamb husbandry, have developed substantial export markets. China, too, is both a major producer of sheep and the world's largest importer of their meat. Whether a grilled chop or a hand-knitted wool sweater, demand for sheep products has never been greater.

In order to learn who is training the next generation of sheep farmers, I headed up to the Stone Barns Center for Food and Agriculture, just north of New York City. This demonstration farm and fine dining restaurant (called Blue Hill at Stone Barns) form a campus where people from all over the world who are concerned with the future of farming can learn about what it can be like. Once there, I met Craig Haney, the resident sheep expert, and discussed the future of sheep

Feta cheese, a very popular sheep's milk product.

farming. Haney had the looks of an archetypical American farmer and the manner of an outgoing schoolteacher. His entire life has been a combination of the two: growing up in farm country, studying history at university and then going on to farm at a living history museum. Haney joined Stone Barns when it opened in 2004, and has been raising sheep there ever since.

Haney began farming not with meat, but with fibre. Wool can do all the useful things that polyester can, except that wool is not made from oil. Haney went on to remind us that not only can sheep be raised on tiny patches of land, but they can produce useful products throughout their lives. The sheep can do far more than we ask it to.

Haney was deeply concerned with the notion of foodsheds. As the world's population grows and redistributes, not only are we finding ourselves facing all sorts of new problems with food supply, but we have to coin new words to describe them. The term foodshed describes an area from which a given place draws its food supply. Vast foodsheds mean increased energy consumption and more easily disrupted supply chains; this adds up to food that costs more to transport than to produce. This is where lamb comes in: sheep are the most efficient producers in the livestock world. As we have seen, they can be raised in close proximity to major cities.

Hand in hand with the idea of the foodshed is that of food security. This is a measure of how accessible food supplies are to the population of a given place. That is, a place has high food security if its people do not fear going hungry. Lamb plays an important role here, too. Sheep can be raised on land that is not suitable for crops, and their milk, meat and fibre can contribute to local economies. You cannot shear a cow, or milk a chicken.

When it comes to lamb, a revolution will not be required if we are to make big changes for the world's small farmers.

A plate of *stobhach,* or Irish Stew, prepared from a 19th-century recipe.

In the United States, a 1 lb (450 g) per person per year increase would save and empower hundreds – if not thousands – of small farms. It is the same in Continental Europe. If most households ate one more meal of lamb each month there would affect local agriculture in an equally profound way. It is a big job, but lamb is up to the task.

Recipes

Bamya (Egyptian Lamb and Okra Stew)

Lamb and okra, two of the most ancient ingredients in Egyptian cuisine, are combined here to make a traditional stew. And please, don't be afraid of okra – if it is slimy, that means it is undercooked, not spoiled, unpleasant or otherwise bad.

3 tbsp vegetable oil
1 tsp ground coriander
1 tsp ground cardamom
1 cup (125 g) chopped onion
4 cloves garlic, crushed and chopped
1½ lb (700 g) lamb stewing meat, cut into 1-inch (2.5-cm) cubes
2 cups (480 ml) canned chopped tomato
½ tsp salt
½ tsp freshly ground black pepper
2 cups (240 g) whole okra

Mix the oil, coriander and cardamom together in a large pot over medium-high heat and cook until the spices are coated with oil, about 1 minute. Reduce the heat to medium and mix in the onion and garlic; cook and stir until the onion is translucent, about 10 minutes. Add the lamb and cook, stirring occasionally, until it is well browned, about 10 minutes. Add the tomato, salt, pepper and 1 cup (240 ml) water, cover the pot and simmer, stirring occasionally, until the lamb becomes tender, about 1 hour.* Reduce the heat to medium-low and mix in the okra. Cook, stirring occasionally, until the okra becomes tender, about 20 minutes. The dish is ready when both the lamb and the okra are very tender and easy to eat. Serve warm with rice.

Serves 4

*If you use boneless lamb, the cooking time will be shorter and you will need only 1 lb (450 g) of lamb.

Basque Lamb Stew

Because the Basques are traditionally shepherds, lamb stew in the region is more of a genre than a specific dish. I have chosen to offer this recipe out of the many available because its simplicity speaks of the remoteness of the shepherd's life.

2 tbsp lard

1 tsp paprika

1 tsp salt

½ tsp freshly ground black pepper

2 lb (900 g) boneless lamb stewing meat, cut into 1-inch (2.5-cm) cubes

8 cloves garlic, crushed and chopped

2 cups (320 g) chopped onion

2 medium carrots, cut into 1-inch (2.5-cm) pieces

2 medium potatoes, cut into dice

2 cups (480 ml) white table wine

2 tbsp chopped flat-leaf parsley

Put the lard in a large pot over medium heat and add the paprika, salt and pepper. Stir until the spice is coated with the fat. Add the lamb and stir until it is well browned, about 15 minutes. It must be brown – not grey. Remove the meat from the pot and set aside.

Add the garlic and onion to the pot and cook, stirring occasionally, until the onion turns translucent and starts to brown at the edges, about 20 minutes. Mix in the carrots and potatoes and cook 5 minutes more. Return the meat to the vegetable mixture, add the wine and 2 cups (480 ml) of water, reduce the heat to medium-low and simmer, uncovered, stirring occasionally, until the meat is fork-tender and the liquid has reduced by half, about an hour. Mix in the parsley and serve hot.

Serves 4

Note: Originally, liver was an essential part of the dish, but – like most Basque cooks today – I am leaving it out. However, if you want to, you can brown a piece of lamb's liver by adding it to the lard and paprika at the start of the recipe. When it is browned, take it out of the pot, set it aside, cut it into small pieces and return it to the stew 1 minute before you are ready to take it off the heat.

Bheja Fry (Indian Curried Lamb Brains)

I think this is the food that visitors to India – and many Indians themselves – fear the most. Organ meat, spice and frying: quite a combination. Yet, for those in the know, it is a delicious treat, with an unctuous texture and vivid flavour combined in a way that most of us are not used to.

1 tbsp cider vinegar
1 tbsp plus 1 tsp salt, divided
¾ lb (350 g) lamb brains (about 3 or 4 whole brains), washed carefully
2 tbsp ghee or butter
4 fresh or dried curry leaves
1 cup (160 g) chopped onion
1 tbsp ginger garlic paste, available at Indian shops
1 tsp hot chilli powder
½ tsp ground cumin
1 tsp ground cardamom
1 tsp ground coriander

¼ tsp ground fenugreek
1 cup (240 ml) chopped fresh tomatoes

Put 2 quarts (1.9 l) of cold water in a pot and add the vinegar, larger quantity of salt and brains. Cover the pot and place over high heat. Bring the liquid to the boil and let it boil for 1 minute. Remove from the heat. Drain the brains and set aside. Discard the liquid. When they are cool enough to touch, chop the brains into thumbnail-sized pieces.

Put the ghee in a frying pan (skillet) over medium-low heat, add the curry leaves, onion and ginger garlic paste, and cook, stirring until the onion is soft and translucent, about 15 minutes. Add the chilli powder, cumin, cardamom, coriander, fenugreek and 1 tsp of salt and stir continuously until the spices coat the onion and there is no powdery texture remaining, about 1 minute. Mix in the tomato and ½ cup (120 ml) of water and cook, stirring occasionally, until the tomato has broken down and combined with the onion and spices, about 20 minutes.

Mix in the cooked brain pieces and cook with occasional stirring until the brains are well-done, about 10 minutes. Serve straight away as part of an Indian meal with naan, chapatis or basmati rice.

Serves 2

Lamb Shanks Braised in Tomato Sauce

At the start of the 1990s, most people had never heard of lamb shanks. Ten years later, those shanks were among the most prized of cuts. This recipe is typical of the sort that made the lamb shank popular. The meat is cooked in a sauce like a stew, but kept whole and on the bone for added flavour. With this long, slow cooking, the connective tissue that might have made the meat tough under other circumstances dissolves and thickens the sauce nicely.

2 tbsp olive oil
2 lamb shanks (about 1½ lb/700 g)
1 tsp dried thyme
1 tsp dried oregano
1 tsp dried rosemary
1 tsp freshly ground black pepper
2 cups (320 g) sliced onion
6 cloves garlic, crushed and chopped
1 cup (240 ml) red wine
2 cups (480 ml) canned crushed tomato or passata
1 tbsp capers, rinsed and drained
salt, to taste

Place the oil and lamb shanks in a casserole dish (Dutch oven) over medium-high heat and cook, turning the meat occasionally, until the meat is well-browned, about 10 minutes. Set the meat aside but do not clean or drain the pan.

Return the pan to the heat and lower the temperature to medium. Add in the thyme, oregano, rosemary and pepper and cook, stirring until you can smell the spices, about 1 minute. Mix in the onion and garlic and cook, stirring, until the onions turn translucent and begin to brown, about 10 minutes.

Reduce the heat to medium-low and mix in the wine, passata, capers and 1 cup (240 ml) of water. When everything is well combined, put the lamb shanks back in the pot. Simmer, covered, until the lamb is tender enough to pull apart with a fork, about 2 hours. You will need to turn the shanks 3 or 4 times while simmering, but otherwise they just cook by themselves.

Taste the sauce. If it needs the extra salt, add it, otherwise it is ready to eat. Serve with rice or polenta.

Serves 2

Braised Leg of Mutton

Cooking mutton well is not easy. The secrets are plenty of time, a good meat thermometer and a big, covered pot.

4 cups (600 g) sliced onion
3 heads garlic, unpeeled and cut in half
1 tbsp dried rosemary
1 tbsp dried oregano
1 tsp dried thyme
1 tbsp salt
1 tbsp freshly ground black pepper
1 whole bone-in leg of mutton (about 8 lb/3.5 kg)
2 bottles dry red wine

Cover the bottom of a roasting tin with the onion slices and garlic pieces in an even layer. Dust the rosemary, oregano, thyme and pepper over the onions and garlic and place the leg of mutton on top. Then pour in one bottle of wine, give it a good shake so that the wine soaks through to the bottom, and put the pot in a cold oven. Bake, covered, at 225°F (110°C/gas mark 1) until a meat thermometer inserted at the thickest point of the meat reads 160°F (71°C), about 6 hours. Turn the meat every hour or so to help it cook evenly. If the mixture gets too dry, add wine, 1 cup (240 ml) at a time, until there is enough liquid to cover the onions easily and provide moisture to cook the meat.

When it is done, remove it from the oven and let it rest at room temperature for about 20 minutes. Carve and serve as if it were a giant leg of lamb (which it is, of course).

Serves 8

Chelo Kebabs (Iranian Lamb Skewers)

This is the national dish of Iran: a simple kebab with minced lamb and Middle Eastern spices that can be eaten as anything from street food to a formal meal. It is welcome wherever it shows up.

2 lb (900 g) ground (minced) lamb
3 eggs
1 cup (180 g) finely chopped onion
2 tsp ground turmeric
½ tsp ground cinnamon
2 tsp sumac
½ tsp salt
1 tsp freshly ground black pepper

Combine the lamb, eggs, onion, turmeric, cinnamon, sumac, salt and pepper in a large bowl and mix until all the ingredients are evenly distributed. Form the mixture into patties the shape and size of a flattened hot dog and let rest in the refrigerator for at least 1 hour. Skewer them if you wish.

Cook the meat on a very hot grill until the outside is well browned, about 3 minutes on each side. Alternatively, bake in the oven at 375°F (190°C/gas mark 5) for 40 minutes or until the meat is well-browned and cooked through. Serve with basmati rice and a knob (pat) of butter.

Makes 8 kebabs; serves approx. 4

Indian Dry Lamb Curry

This dish is dry compared to the curries that most of us know, but not dry in the way a completely sauce-less grilled lamb chop would be. The powerful marinade becomes a very delicious sauce.

1 large onion, roughly chopped
1-inch (2.5-cm) piece of fresh ginger, peeled
8 cloves garlic
1 tsp ground cumin
1 tsp freshly ground black pepper
2 tsp ground coriander
½ tsp garam masala
½ tsp salt

1 tsp turmeric
1 lb (450 g) lamb stewing meat, cut into 1-inch (2.5-cm) cubes
2 tbsp vegetable oil
2 tbsp fresh hot green chillies, sliced
8 curry leaves, torn into small pieces

Combine the onion, ginger and garlic in a food processor and blend into a thick paste. Add the cumin, pepper, coriander, garam masala, salt and turmeric and process until the spices are evenly blended.

Put the onion-and-spice mixture and the lamb in a large bowl and mix wel until the meat is completely coated. Cover and leave to marinate in the refrigerator for at least 1 hour.

Put the oil and chilli into a large frying pan (skillet) over medium heat and cook, stirring occasionally, until the chilli starts to brown at the edges, about 5 minutes. Mix in the marinated lamb and continue to cook, until the meat is cooked through and the sauce is no longer bitter, about 30 minutes. Add the curry leaves and cook, stirring, for 1 minute more. Serve straight away as part of an Indian meal.

Serves 4

Limburgse Stoofpot Van Lamsvlees
(Dutch Lamb Stew)

Dutch cooking is so unsung that despite having visited the country several times, I couldn't name a single cooked dish. Now I know their lamb stew, and am a better cook for it.

½ cup (75 g) plain (all-purpose) flour
2 tsp dried thyme
½ tsp salt
½ tsp freshly ground black pepper
2 lb (900 g) boneless lamb stewing meat, cut into ½-inch (1-cm) cubes
¼ cup (4 tbsp) olive oil

2 tbsp butter
4 cups (640 g) chopped onion
8 fresh garlic cloves
1 cup (240 ml) canned crushed tomato or passata
2 cups (480 ml) red wine
3 bay leaves
½ cup (115 g) chopped black olives
2 tbsp chopped fresh parsley

Combine the flour, thyme, salt and pepper in a sealable plastic bag and give it a few shakes so as to distribute the ingredients evenly. Put the lamb pieces in the bag and shake until the meat is evenly coated.

Put the olive oil and butter in a casserole dish (Dutch oven) or large saucepan over medium heat and when the butter is melted add the lamb. Cook, turning frequently, until the lamb is golden brown. This may work best in small batches. Remove the meat from the pan and set aside, leaving the pan, juices and all, on the heat.

Add the onions and garlic to the pan and cook, stirring, until the onions become golden brown and the remaining juices from the lamb have loosened and combined with the onions, about 10 minutes. Reduce the heat to low and cook the onion mixture, stirring occasionally, until it is reduced in volume by half, about 40 minutes. Mix in the crushed tomato, wine and bay leaves. Give them a good stir, then add the cooked lamb. Reduce the heat to medium-low, cover and simmer, stirring occasionally, until the lamb is very tender and a sauce has formed, about 1½ hours.

Mix in the chopped olives and parsley and simmer, uncovered, until the olive flavour has blended in, about 10 minutes. Serve hot as a main course.

Serves 4

Note: If you are cooking this ahead of time, keep the olives and parsley separate and add them after you reheat the stew.

Pan-fried Lamb Kidneys

Among the livestock that people commonly consume, the lamb is one of few animals whose kidneys are delicate enough in taste and texture to grill or fry. This presents American consumers with a special problem: these meats are easier for processors to export than sell, making them very hard to find in the u.s. Be persistent at your butcher, though, and he will set aside a few for you that otherwise would have gone to a fine French restaurant.

1 lb (450 g) lamb's kidney (about 4 kidneys)
1 tsp salt
1 tsp freshly ground black pepper
2 tbsp butter

Slice each kidney in half lengthwise and cut out the hard, fatty part. Sprinkle the salt and pepper on both sides.

Melt the butter in a frying pan (skillet) over medium heat and sauté the kidneys until they just begin to brown, about 2 minutes on each side. Serve straight away with a dab of hot mustard.
Serves 2

Navarin Printanier (French Lamb Stew)

For the French, both turnips and lamb are signs of spring, and this stew combines them in a classic way.

½ cup (70 g) plain all-purpose flour
1 tsp salt
1 tsp freshly ground black pepper
2 lb (900 g) boneless lamb stewing meat, cut into 1-inch (2.5-cm) cubes
2 tbsp vegetable oil
1 clove garlic, crushed
1 tsp dried thyme
1 bay leaf

3 cups (700 ml) beef stock (broth)
½ cup (120 ml) canned crushed tomato or passata
1 cup (240 ml) dry white wine
1 bunch baby carrots, cleaned and peeled (try to use the real thing if you can)
2 cups (300 g) chopped red potatoes, chopped
1 cup (150 g) turnip, chopped and peeled
1 cup (190 g) baby (pearl) onions (use fresh if you can find them, otherwise frozen)
1 cup (120 g) green peas (use fresh if you can find them, otherwise frozen)

Combine the flour, salt and pepper in a large, sealable plastic bag. Put small batches of the meat into the bag and shake until it is well coated. Put the oil in a casserole dish (Dutch oven) over high heat and brown the floured meat in small batches. Set the browned meat aside; do not clean the pan. Reduce the heat to medium-low and add the garlic, thyme and bay leaf to the pan. Stir briefly and add the browned meat, stock (broth), crushed tomato, wine, carrots, potatoes and turnip. Simmer, covered, stirring occasionally, until the pieces of lamb start to become tender, about 40 minutes.

Mix in the onions and peas and simmer until all the vegetables are tender, about 20 more minutes. Remove the bay leaf and serve immediately.

Serves 4

Gyros (Greek-style Grilled Lamb Patties)

This dish combines minced lamb with seasonings to make patties with really classic Greek flavours – nothing like the great blobs of grey paste you see roasting on a spit in kebab shops.

1 large onion, roughly chopped
3 cloves garlic
2 lb (900 g) minced (ground) lamb
2 tsp salt

1 tsp freshly ground black pepper
2 tsp ground cumin
2 tsp dried oregano
1 tsp ground nutmeg
1 tsp dried rosemary
1 tsp dried thyme
oil, or oil spray, for the grill pan

Combine the onions and garlic in a food processor and pulse until reduced to a fine mash. Remove from the processor and strain through a colander lined with muslin (cheesecloth). Press or squeeze the onion/garlic mash to remove any remaining liquid.

In a large bowl, combine the onion/garlic mash, lamb, salt, pepper, cumin, oregano, nutmeg, rosemary and thyme, and mix well. Though a wooden spoon or potato masher might do the job, I find that hands work best here. When the spices are evenly distributed, cover in cling film (plastic wrap), put in the refrigerator and let stand for at least 1 hour so the flavours can combine.

Form the meat mixture into patties and cook on a well-oiled grill pan over high heat, turning over once so that both sides are cooked, about 7 minutes per side. Grill until the meat is cooked and dark-brown char marks have formed. Serve straight away with tzatziki, the classic yogurt and cucumber dip, or hot sauce.
Serves 4

Hunan Lamb

Back in the 1970s, this dish suddenly appeared on the menus of Chinese restaurants all over America. It was part of the Sichuan/Hunan food revolution of that era. For old-timers, it was a bit of a surprise to see lamb return to the Chinese menu; for everybody else, new spicy dishes like this one were a welcome change.

1 lb (450 g) boneless lamb stewing meat
¼ cup (4 tbsp) soy sauce
¼ cup (4 tbsp) Chinese rice wine

1 tsp sugar
3 tbsp peanut oil
3–6 whole dried Sichuan chillies
1 tbsp minced fresh ginger
3 cloves garlic, crushed and finely chopped
1 cup (90 g) spring onions (scallions) or Chinese leeks, cut into
2-inch (5-cm) pieces

Place the lamb in the freezer for 20–30 minutes. This firms it up and makes it easier to slice. Then slice the meat into thin strips about ⅛ inch (0.25 cm) thick and 1 inch (2.5 cm) long.

Combine the soy sauce, rice wine and sugar in a large bowl and add the lamb strips. Stir to coat the meat evenly. Leave to marinate in the refrigerator for at least 1 hour.

Put a wok on your hottest burner, add the oil and let it heat up. It should be as hot as you can get it for stir-frying. Add the chillies, ginger and garlic and cook, stirring, until the garlic starts to brown, about 1 minute. Mix in the marinated meat and keep cooking, stirring constantly, until they start to brown, about 3 minutes. Add the spring onions (scallions) and keep cooking until they become tender, about 2 minutes. Give the mixture one last toss and serve straight away, with rice.

Serves 4

Khoresht-e Aloo
(Iranian Lamb Stewed With Prunes)

Just when you have finally convinced your friends to try lamb, along comes another challenging ingredient: prunes. Prunes have such a bad rep that they even tried to change their name to 'dried plums'.

¼ cup (4 tbsp) clarified butter or ghee
2 lb (900 g) lamb stewing meat, cut into 1-inch (2.5-cm) cubes
1 tsp ground turmeric
½ tsp ground cinnamon

2 cups (320 g) chopped onion
2 cups (480 ml) chicken stock (broth)
½ tsp salt
1 tsp freshly ground black pepper
1 cup (230 g) stoned (pitted) prunes
¼ cup (4 tbsp) fresh lime juice
1 tbsp light brown sugar

Put the butter in a heavy pot over medium-high heat and brown the lamb pieces. They'll need several minutes on each side. When they are done, remove them from the pot and set aside. (Some people find it easier to brown the meat in small batches.)

Reduce the heat to medium-low and mix in the turmeric, cinnamon and onion. Cook, stirring occasionally, until the onion has turned translucent and begun to brown at the edges, about 20 minutes. Add the stock (broth), salt and pepper and return the browned lamb to the pot. Simmer, covered, stirring occasionally, until the meat starts to become tender, about 1 hour.

Add the prunes, lime juice and brown sugar. Cover and simmer, stirring occasionally, until the prunes are well-cooked and the meat is completely tender, about 30 more minutes. Serve straight away, with basmati rice.

Serves 4

Stobhach (Irish Stew)

I thought I knew what Irish stew was: beef, potatoes and carrots in a thick, herby brown sauce with a bit of Guinness stout added for depth. Boy, was I wrong! What I remember should really be called 'American stew'. The real thing – just called 'stew' in Ireland – is made with lamb by most people and with mutton by real stew purists. Originally, it contained just mutton, onions, parsley and salt. Here we bring it up to the nineteenth century with the inclusion of potatoes and carrots.

2 lb (900 g) bone-in mutton stewing meat
1 tsp salt
2 cups (300 g) onions, quartered
2 cups (280 g) carrots, peeled and cut into 1-inch (2.5-cm) pieces
2 cups (300 g) potato, peeled and cut into 1-inch pieces
½ cup (120 ml) chopped parsley

Place the meat and salt in a large pot along with 8 cups (1.9 l) of cold water. Cover the pot and place over medium-low heat. Cook, stirring occasionally, until the meat is fork-tender, about 3 hours. If scum or foam forms, skim it off.

Mix in the onion, carrot, potato and parsley and cook, stirring occasionally, until the potatoes are very tender, about 1 hour. If there is too much liquid, remove the cover and let some water evaporate. If it is too dry, add water until the meat and vegetables are barely covered.

Serve with bread and Irish stout. Non-purists might want to add a drop of hot sauce or a spoonful of mustard, too.

Serves 4

Lamb Bouillon using Ingredients from the Larsa Tablet

There are too many unanswered questions to call this an actual Mesopotamian dish. It seems unlikely that the Mesopotamians ate only the meat of the sheep in the way that we do. There would almost certainly have been blood and organ meat in the recipe, too. Cooking times are unknown and would be very different from those used to cook modern lamb. And note that, while the name has been translated by scholars as 'bouillon', it is not a broth as we know it, but rather a rich, almost porridge-like stew. With all those missing details in mind, let's take an educated guess.

2 tbsp lard or cooking oil
1 cup (160 g) chopped onion
1 tbsp whole cumin seeds

1 cup (180 g) sliced leeks, including a bit of the greens
3 cloves garlic, crushed and chopped
1 tsp salt
1 lb (450 g) bone-in lamb stewing meat
1 cup (240 ml) whole wheat berries, soaked for at least 24 hours, then drained

Put the lard or oil, onion, cumin seeds, leeks, garlic and salt in a large pot over medium heat. Cook and stir until the onions are translucent and browned at the edges, about 10 minutes. Mix in the lamb and cook, stirring occasionally, until the meat is browned, about 20 minutes. Increase the heat to high, then add 5 cups (1.2 l) of water and the soaked wheat berries, and bring the entire mixture to the boil. Allow the pot to boil for 1 minute, then reduce the heat to medium-low and simmer, stirring occasionally, until the meat is very tender, about 90 minutes. Serve as a soup in bowls.
Serves 4

Pan-fried Lamb's Testicles

Do you want them fried in lard the way Lorenzo Magalotti (pp. 50–51) liked them? Or maybe in olive oil, the way most people would eat them today. Either way, they're rich, filled with flavour and guaranteed to be a very big surprise at any dinner party.

2 lb (900 g) lamb's testicles
1 cup (70 g) plain (all-purpose) flour
1 tsp salt
1 tsp freshly ground black pepper
2 tbsp olive oil*

*True food-history fanatics will use lard instead; if you do, make sure the lard you choose is not hydrogenated.

Peel the testicles. The easiest way is first to locate the edge of the outer membrane, then score it with a knife. You should then be able to insert a finger between the meat and the membrane and, with that, the outer will come off in one piece. When they are peeled, slice the meat into 1-inch (2.5 cm) pieces.

Combine the flour, salt and pepper in a bowl. Dredge the meat in the flour so that it is evenly coated.

Put the oil in a frying pan (skillet) over medium-high heat and fry the testicle pieces. Turn them over in the pan and make sure they're cooked all the way through and on both sides. Serve straight away with a squeeze of lemon and hot sauce.

Serves 4

'Mongolian' Lamb Hotpot

If you ask anybody who knows their Chinese food, they will tell you that this dish is called a 'Mongolian hotpot'. The only problem is that while there might be some Mongolian in the cooking technique, it is as Chinese as can be. Serve it for dinner and expect plenty of cheer from adults and a big mess from children. Anything and everything you need for this recipe – including the hotpot itself – is available at your local Chinese grocery shop for less than the cost of a good restaurant meal.

8 cups (1.9 l) mild chicken stock (broth)
1 tbsp Chinese cooking wine
1 tbsp soy sauce
3 slices fresh ginger root, each about the size of a penny
3 cloves garlic, crushed
1 lb (450 g) boneless lamb, thinly sliced for hotpot cooking*
¼ cup (4 tbsp) Chinese hot chilli paste
8 oz (225 g) tofu, cut into dice-sized cubes
1 cup (150 g) bean sprouts
8 oz (225 g) uncooked Chinese wheat noodles

*Look for it in the frozen meat section of an Asian supermarket. You can also find beef and pork cut this way if you so choose.

Put your electric hotpot in the centre of the serving table, add the stock (broth), wine, soy sauce, ginger and garlic, and plug the pot in. Let the liquid simmer, stirring occasionally, for at least 1 hour. Add water if the broth evaporates.

When your guests are seated around the hotpot, place the raw sliced meat on the table and put a small plate, some chopsticks and a soup bowl in front of each person. Put the hot sauce out, too.

Encourage your guests to cook the slices of lamb by dipping them into the simmering broth. If they are hesitant, throw some slices in yourself. The meat will be ready to eat in a matter of seconds: retrieve it with chopsticks, dip it in the hot sauce and eat straight away. If the liquid evaporates before people everyone is finished cooking and eating, add more water to bring the level back up.

When the meat is finished, add the tofu, bean sprouts and noodles to the simmering broth (now beautifully flavoured by the lamb). Cook, stirring occasionally, until the noodles are tender, about 8 minutes. Serve straight away and don't forget to unplug the hotpot as soon as the broth is finished.

Serves 4

Plov (Uzbek Lamb with Rice)

This big pot of lamb, rice and vegetables (and plenty of garlic) is one of the great festive dishes of Uzbekistan. Make it where a one-pot meal or complete main dish is in order. And whatever you do, don't leave out the garlic!

2 tbsp vegetable oil
1 lb (450 g) boneless lamb stewing meat, cut into 1-inch
(2.5-cm) cubes
2 cups (300 g) thinly sliced onion
1 cup (125 g) shredded carrot
2 heads garlic, rinsed but not peeled
1 tbsp whole cumin seeds

1 tbsp whole coriander seeds
¼ cup (4 tbsp) dried barberries
1 cup (200 g) basmati rice, rinsed and drained
1 tsp salt

Put the oil in a pot over high heat and add the lamb. Cook, stirring, until the meat is browned – not grey – about 5 minutes. Remove the meat, set it aside and lower the heat to medium-low.

Add the onions to the now-empty pot and cook, stirring, until the onions have absorbed the browned bits of lamb from the bottom of the pot, turned translucent and started to brown at the edges, about 20 minutes. Mix in the carrot, garlic heads – yes, put them in whole – cumin seeds, coriander seeds, barberries, browned meat and 1½ cups (350 ml) of water and cook, covered, stirring occasionally, until the lamb is tender, about 35 minutes.

Raise the heat to high, add 1½ cups (350 ml) of water and bring it to the boil. Give it an occasional stir while it is heating up so that nothing sticks, and when the water is boiling, add the rice and salt. Make sure all the ingredients are evenly distributed with a few last stirs, reduce the heat to medium-low, cover, and let cook without disturbing until the rice has absorbed the liquid, about 20 minutes. Serve straight away and make sure each diner gets some garlic.

Serves 4

Zhua Fan (Xinjiang Lamb Rice)

This is one of the most puzzling recipes I've ever come across. It is Chinese, Uzbek and maybe Uighur too. It is a rice pot, a pilaf or maybe even a remote cousin of a biryani. And with Sichuan pepper, soy sauce and cumin, it bridges at least two cultures.

2 tbsp peanut oil
2 tsp Sichuan peppercorns
1 tsp ground cumin
1 tsp freshly ground black pepper

2½ lb (1.1 kg) bone-in lamb shoulder*
1 cup (150 g) coarsely chopped white or yellow onion
1 cup (150 g) sliced carrot
1 cup (120 g) sliced or chopped shiitake mushrooms
2 tbsp soy sauce
2 cups (420 g) short-grain white rice

*It is easier to debone the lamb once it is cooked.

Put the oil, peppercorns, cumin and black pepper in a large pot over medium-high heat and cook, stirring, until the spices are evenly mixed into the oil, about 1 minute. Add the lamb shoulder to the pot and cook, turning occasionally, until the meat is well browned, about 15 minutes. Remove the meat from the pot and set aside.

Leaving the residue of meat, spice and oil in the pot, add the onion, carrot, mushroom and soy sauce and cook, stirring, until the onions begin to brown, about 5 minutes. Increase the heat to high, add 6 cups (1.4 l) of water and the browned meat, and bring to the boil. When the pot has boiled for 1 minute, reduce the heat to medium-low, cover and let simmer, stirring occasionally, until the meat is falling off the bone, about 1.5 hours. Remove the meat from the pot one more time and set aside.

Increase the heat to high, bring the liquid to the boil and add the rice. Stir a few times to mix the rice in evenly, then reduce the heat to medium-low, cover and let cook until the rice absorbs the liquid, about 25 minutes. Turn off the heat.

Remove the lamb meat from the bone and place it in a layer on top of the cooked rice and vegetables. Let it stand for 5 minutes or so to warm the meat. Discard the bone. Serve immediately.

Serves 4

Select Bibliography

Achaya, K. T., *Indian Food: A Historical Companion* (New Delhi, 1994)

Albala, Ken, *Eating Right in the Renaissance* (Berkeley, CA, 2002)

Anderson, E. N., *The Food of China* (New Haven, CT, 1988)

Arberry, A. J., Charley Perry and Maxime Rodinson, *Medieval Arab Cookery* (Totnes, 2001)

Bencini, Walter, *The Women of Zeri*, DVD (Chicago and Montevarchi, 2009)

Berriedale-Johnson, Michelle, *Food Fit for Pharaohs: An Ancient Egyptian Cookbook* (London, 1999)

Blatner, David, and Rabbi Ted Falcon, *Judaism for Dummies* (New York, 2001)

Bober, Phyllis Pray, *Art, Culture, and Cuisine: Ancient and Medieval Gastronomy* (London, 1999)

Bradshaw, George, *Bradshaw's Hand-book to the Turkish Empire* (Manchester, 1876)

Bruni, Frank, 'Where the Lore is Part of the Lure', www.newyorktimes.com, 14 December 2005

Campbell, Helen, *In Foreign Kitchens* (Boston, MA, 1893)

Campo, Juan E., *Encyclopedia of Islam* (New York, 2009)

Camporesi, Piero, *Exotic Brew: The Art of Living in the Age of Enlightenment* (Cambridge, 1990)

——, *The Magic Harvest: Food, Folklore and Society* (Cambridge, 1993)

Chang, K. C., *Food in Chinese Culture: Anthropological and Historical Perspectives* (New Haven, CT, 1977)

Coe, Andrew, *Chop Suey: A Cultural History of Chinese Food in the United States* (Oxford, 2009)

The Compleat English and French Cook (London, 1674)

Conkling, Alfred R., *Appletons' Guide to Mexico* (New York, 1891)

Cooper, Joseph, *The Art of Cookery Refin'd and Augmented* (London, 1654)

Courtine, Robert J., and Celine Vence, *The Grand Masters of French Cuisine: Five Centuries of Great Cooking* (New York, 1978)

Dalby, Andrew, *Siren Feasts: A History of Food and Gastronomy in Greece* (London, 1996)

Davidis, Henriette, *German National Cookery for American Kitchens* (Milwaukee, WI, 1904)

De Voe, Thomas F., *The Market Book* (New York, 1862)

Del Conte, Anna, *Gastronomy of Italy* (London, 2002)

DeRoma, Julius, and Peter Holbrook, *Kitchen Conquests of Ancient Rome* (Minneapolis, MN, 1975)

Dickens, Charles, *Household Words: A Weekly Journal* (March–September 1850)

Dickson Wright, Clarissa, and Jennifer Paterson, *Two Fat Ladies: Gastronomic Adventures (with Motorbike and Sidecar)* (London, 1996)

Fearnley-Whittingstall, Hugh, *The River Cottage Cookbook* (London, 2001)

Glasse, Hannah, *The Art of Cookery Made Plain and Easy* (London, 1784)

Grabhorn, Robert, *A Commonplace Book of Cookery* (San Francisco, CA, 1985)

Grottanelli, Cristiano, and Lucio Milano, eds, *Food and Identity in the Ancient World* (Padua, 2004)

Henderson, Fergus, *The Whole Beast: Nose to Tail Eating* (New York, 2004)

Hess, Karen, *Martha Washington's Booke of Cookery* (New York, 1981)

Lawson, Nigella, *Feast: Food that Celebrates Life* (New York, 2004)

Lewicka, Paulina B., *Food and Foodways of Medieval Cairenes* (Leiden, 2011)

McDaniel, Jan, *The Food of Mexico* (Philadelphia, PA, 2003)

Montanari, Massimo, and Alberto Capatti, *Italian Cuisine: A Cultural History* (New York, 1999)

Murray, John, *A Handbook for Travellers in Egypt* (London, 1875)

Newman, Jacqueline M., *Food Culture in China* (Westport, CT, 2004)

Paston-Williams, Sara, *The Art of Dining: A History of Cooking and Eating* (London, 1993)

Pei-Mei, Fu, *Pei-Mei's Chinese Cookbook*, vol. 1 (Taipei, 1969)

Perrier, Amelia, *A Winter in Morocco* (London, 1873)

Pilcher, Jeffrey M., *Que vivan los tamales! Food and the Making of Mexican Identity* (Albuquerque, NM, 1998)

Psilakis, Michael, *How to Roast a Lamb: New Greek Classic Cooking* (New York, 2009)

Riley, Gillian, *The Oxford Companion to Italian Food* (Oxford, 2007)

Rose, Peter G., *The Sensible Cook: Dutch Foodways in the Old and the New World* (Syracuse, NY, 1989)

Ross, Deborah, *The Manischewitz Passover Cookbook* (New York, 1969)

Rushworth, Dr William A., *The Sheep* (Buffalo, NY, 1899)

Samuelsson, Marcus, *The Soul of a New Cuisine: A Discovery of the Foods and Flavors of Africa* (Hoboken, NJ, 2006)

Scully, D. Eleanor, and Terence Scully, *Early French Cookery: Sources, History, Original Recipes and Modern Adaptations* (Ann Arbor, MI, 1995)

Scully, Terence, *The Neapolitan Recipe Collection: Cuoco Napoletano* (Ann Arbor, MI, 2000)

Segan, Francine, *The Philosopher's Kitchen: Recipes from Ancient Greece and Rome for the Modern Cook* (New York, 2004)

Simoons, Frederick J., *Food in China: A Cultural and Historical Inquiry* (Boca Raton, FL, 1991)

Sing Au, M., *The Chinese Cook Book* (Reading, PA, 1936)

Slow Food Foundation for Biodiversity, *The Ark of Taste*, www.slowfoodfoundation.com/ark, accessed 24 May 2012

Solomon, Jon, and Julia Solomon, *Ancient Roman Feasts and Recipes Adapted for Modern Cooking* (Miami, FL, 1977)

Soyer, Alexis, *The Pantropheon; or, History of Food, and its Preparation . . .* (Boston, MA, 1863)

Tannahill, Reay, *Food in History* (New York, 1988)

Tapper, Richard, and Sami Zubaida, *A Taste of Thyme: Culinary Cultures of the Middle East* (London, 2000)

Toussaint-Samat, Maguelonne, *A History of Food* (Chichester, 2009)

Tsai, Ming, *Blue Ginger* (New York, 1999)

Ude, Louis Eustache, *The French Cook: A System of Fashionable and Economical Cookery Adapted to the Use of English Families* (London, 1829)

Waines, David, *In a Caliph's Kitchen* (London, 1989)

Waters, Alice, *Chez Panisse Menu Cookbook* (New York, 1982)

Weiss Adamson, Melitta, ed., *Regional Cuisines of Medieval Europe: A Book of Essays* (New York, 2002)

Wilkins, John, *The Boastful Chef: The Discourse of Food in Ancient Greek Comedy* (Oxford, 2000)

Wilkins, John, David Harvey and Michael J. Dobson, eds, *Food in Antiquity: Studies in Ancient Society and Culture* (Exeter, 1995)

Willard, Pat, *America Eats!* (New York, 2008)

Witherspoon, Gary, 'Sheep in Navajo Culture and Social Organization', *American Anthropologist*, LXXVII/5 (October 1973), pp. 1141–8

Wolfe, Linda, *The Literary Gourmet: Menus from Masterpieces* (New York, 1985)

Ziegelman, Jane, *97 Orchard: An Edible History of Five Immigrant Families in One New York Tenement* (New York, 2010)

Websites and Associations

General

Fans of Lamb
www.fansoflamb.com

Mutton Renaissance
www.muttonrenaissance.org.uk

Sheep 101
www.sheep101.info

Associations

American Sheep Industry Association
www.sheepusa.org

Irish Cattle and Sheep Farmers' Association
www.icsaireland.ie

Meat and Livestock Australia
www.australian-lamb.com

National Sheep Association (UK)
www.nationalsheep.org.uk

Navajo-Churro Sheep Association
www.navajo-churrosheep.com

New Zealand Sheepbreeders Association
www.nzsheep.co.nz

Festivals

The Australian Sheep and Wool Show
www.sheepshow.com

Hantam Meat Festival (South Africa)
www.hantamvleisfees.co.za

Kirtlington Lamb Ale Morris Festival (Oxfordshire, UK)
www.kirtlington-morris.org.uk/kirtlington-lamb-ale-2

Kótelettan BBQ Festival (Iceland)
www.kotelettan.is

Maryland Sheep and Wool Festival (USA)
www.sheepandwool.org

Roscommon Lamb Festival (Ireland)
www.roscommonlambfestival.com

Zhuanghang Summer Mutton Festival (Shanghai)
http://english.fengxian.gov.cn/travel5.asp

Lamb Restaurants

Little Sheep Mongolian Hotpot (Asia and North America)
www.littlesheephotpot.com

Acknowledgements

First there are the farmers; Shelly Nussbaum, Hisham Moharram and Torrey Reade in New Jersey and Rod Hewitt and Art Herttua in Vermont. These people took me onto their pastures and gave me some good lessons in lamb and sheep husbandry. A couple of experts pitched in too. Drexel University Culinary Instructor Bob del Grosso gave me a good introduction to butchering and valiantly tasted my first roast leg of mutton, and Craig Haney from The Stone Barns Center for Food and Agriculture in Pocantico Hills, New York offered a view of the future of small farming that was encouraging and enlightening. Finally, none of this would have been possible without my use of the Wertheim Study at the New York Public Library. There, I was able to spend many hours researching lamb, sheep, meat and the history behind all of it. Thank you everybody.

Photo Acknowledgements

The author and the publishers wish to express their thanks to the below sources of illustrative material and/or permission to reproduce it.

All images by Brian Yarvin except the following: Alamy: p. 10 (PRISMA ARCHIVO); Bazel: p. 38; © The Trustees of the British Museum: pp. 26, 29; © British Library Board: pp. 19, 44; Corbis: p. 25 (Elio Ciol); Davric: p. 66; JJ Harrison: p. 90; iStockphoto: pp. 6 (Artfoliophoto), 9, 56 (nicoolay), 70 (Artisan); Georges Jansoone JoJan: p. 23; Marie-Lan Nguyen (2006): p. 35; Shutterstock: pp. 14 (Aleksandar Todoorovic), 40 (ChameleonsEye); Victoria & Albert Museum, London: p. 28 bottom.

Index

italic numbers refer to illustrations; **bold** to recipes